ALSO BY ROBERTO HERNANDEZ

The Secret to a Blessed Marriage One Flesh
Reencounter with Jesus

Take Your *Sandals* Off

A Daily Walk in His Presence

ROBERTO HERNANDEZ

WESTBOW·
PRESS
A DIVISION OF THOMAS NELSON
& ZONDERVAN

Unless otherwise indicated, Bible quotations are taken from the New King James Version of the Bible. Copyright 1982 by Thomas Nelson, Inc. Used by permission. All rights reserved.

Scripture quotations marked MSG are taken from The Message by Eugene H. Petersen, copyright © 1993, 1994, 1995, 1996, 2000, 2001, 2002. Used by permission of NavPress Publishing Group. All rights reserved.

Scripture quotations marked NIV are taken from the Holy Bible, New International Version®. Copyright © 1973, 1978, 1984, 2011 by Biblica, Inc. Used by permission. All rights reserved worldwide.

Scripture quotations marked NLT are taken from the Holy Bible, New Living Translation, Copyright © 1996, 2004, 2007. Used by permission of Tyndale House Inc., Carol Stream, Illinois 60188 All rights reserved.

Names and details of some stories have been changed in order to protect the privacy of the individuals involved.

Author Photo by AC Studio Photography

Author Credits: Author of Reencounter With Jesus.

WestBow Press books may be ordered through booksellers or by contacting:

WestBow Press
A Division of Thomas Nelson & Zondervan
1663 Liberty Drive
Bloomington, IN 47403
www.westbowpress.com
1 (866) 928-1240

ISBN: 978-1-4908-8284-0 (sc)
ISBN: 978-1-4908-8286-4 (hc)
ISBN: 978-1-4908-8285-7 (e)

Library of Congress Control Number: 2015908943

Print information available on the last page.

WestBow Press rev. date: 6/9/2015

Contents

Introduction

Many of the inhabitants of our rapidly changing world have made good look bad and bad look good. We are a society that has deviated from the Word of God, proclaiming that the Word (the Holy Bible) contradicts itself, when in reality it is our understanding and our minds that contradict themselves. Most people lack understanding and are not aware that the mysteries of God are not read but revealed by the Spirit who knows all things—past, present, and future.

Many of us long to have a deep personal relationship with the Lord. Sadly, however, we often do not know how to do this. There are many ideas and opinions on how to accomplish this worthy goal, but you know what? Opinions are just opinions. They are just like noses—everyone has one.

A relationship with God is personal. You do not need to base your relationship with Him on someone else's opinion. People's opinions on God are misleading, so get the facts for yourself. Go to the main source by yourself.

Self-help books will not give you the answers you are looking for. They may lead, train, and sometimes equip you on your journey to developing and reinforcing a deeper relationship with God, but if you are not careful, they will mislead you. Seeking God's face is individual; it is an attitude of longing, willingness, and faithfulness. It is an act of surrendering and accepting Him. It's not wrong of us to seek God's power, peace, presence, or glory, but before anything else, we must resolve to do as the psalmist said: "My heart says of you, 'Seek his face!' Your face, LORD, I will seek" (Ps. 27:8 NIV).

You may have accepted Jesus years ago but have not surrendered completely to Him. However when you "take off your sandals"— not just dust them off, but remove them to walk a holy walk with Him—your life will begin to have meaning and purpose. When you finally find Him, He will indeed forgive you of all your sins. He will sanctify you, purify you, empower you, guide you, and use you mightily to bring Him glory. He will give you talents and abilities that you never had before. Your life will be transformed, and you will become newly born in spirit and truth.

You might be serving the body of Christ as a preacher, leader, pastor, or minister. Nonetheless, somehow a battle rages between your ears. Maybe you are living a double life, acting a certain way when people are around and another way when you are alone. You want to believe what you preach, but somehow your beliefs and faith system feel far off. They are empty and unfulfilling.

In this book, you will find ways to deal with the issues of the world and everyday living. Whether you are a leader, minister, pastor, preacher, or servant of the Lord, you will be helped in your journey to walk a holy life, a life separated from the world's system and dedicated to the Lord God. You will learn the meaning of truly serving God. You will gain a deeper understanding of God and the purpose He has for you life.

Many people labor under the misconception that following the Lord is hard. I tell you the truth: it is not hard—it is impossible—when you try to do it alone. But empowered by the Comforter, impossibilities become possibilities for change and transformation by the daily renewing of your mind.

May the Lord shine His light upon you and guide you on your daily walk in His presence.

CHAPTER 1

Divine Order

Tommy was only five years old when I first met him, a smart, polite, and energetic young boy. Over the course of every year, I would see him periodically; somehow I sensed something different about this boy that made me want to build a friendship with him. Every time I saw Tommy, I would talk to him and encourage him. Every time he would see me, he would call my name and say hello.

Tommy shared with me that his parents were not regular churchgoers. His mom identified herself as a Christian Catholic, but she went to a different church from his father, who carried the label of Baptist. Tommy was undecided in his faith, receiving no direction as to which church he should attend. Since his parents were pulling to one side and to the other, he decided not to bother with either.

Divine Appointment

When I was at the park one summer in the early evening, I came across Tommy again. He shared with me that he had just celebrated his thirteenth birthday a few days earlier. He was now taller, but still very polite and respectful. However, one thing was different this time around. Not only did he say hello, but he also placed his hand on my shoulder with a smile on his face and said, "Hey, Rob, how are you doing?"

"I'm well, thank you," I responded. "How are you doing?"

"Great, thank you," he replied.

"That is awesome," I answered. Then I turned toward his twelve-year-old friend who was hanging out with him and said to both of them, "Staying out of trouble?"

"Yeah," they responded.

"How about church?" Turning my eyes towards Tommy, I asked, "You go to church, Tom?"

"No," he answered.

"Why?" I questioned him. "What? They . . . they don't let you in?"

He smiled and said, "No, silly. Of course, they let me in, but the reason I don't go is because there is too much religion in church."

I thought to myself, *A thirteen-year-old telling me this!* Speaking out loud, I agreed with him and said, "Don't put your mind on religion. Seek a relationship with God instead." Then I added, "Do you understand how God operates?"

Tommy answered, "What do you mean?"

"Well," I explained, "you probably hear all the time about the Trinity—God the Father, God the Son, and God the Holy Spirit."

"Oh yeah, I know about that," he responded.

"Do you understand how God is in the Trinity? Come on— let me share with you about the Lord and some of the mysteries of the kingdom of God."

I took some time and began to tell the boys about God and how the Trinity operates. I used a bottle of water as an example, saying, "Let's say that this water represents God; then let's take the water and put it into a freezer. What happens with the water then?" I asked them.

They replied, "It turns into ice."

"Exactly," I agreed. "Now, the ice represents Jesus. You can see it, and you can hold it. It is the same water as before, but it is in a different state, doing a different function."

I continued: "Let's take the same water and boil it. What happens to the water now?" They said together, "It evaporates."

"Exactly!" I exclaimed. "It evaporates. It turns into 'air.' God the Holy Spirit is like the air—He is everywhere." Then I inhaled some air and said, "That is why we say that God is in us."

Surprised and amazed, Tommy looked at me and said, "You mean we are gods?"

As soon as I heard that I wanted to laugh out loud, but I didn't want to make him uncomfortable, so I just smiled and said, "No we are not gods. It's just that God lives in us—His Spirit is with us, in us, and for us."

I then said, "Let me give you a book so you can have a better understanding of God." I gave him a copy of my book *Reencounter with Jesus* and said, "Read it, and then let's get in touch. If you have any questions, please let me know."

I was open to sharing the love, power, sovereignty, mercy, grace, and transcendence of God with the two boys. I realized they were hungry for the truth and had found in me someone to share it with them. Talking out loud, I began to explain.

"The whole story started when the Lord God created all things in six days. In the Bible, we learn that the Trinity was at work before the foundation of the world. There in the beginning of creation, we learn about the creator God, who made all things. We learn about the Word, who is Jesus, through whom everything was created. We also learn about the Holy Spirit, that when God our Father made man and 'breathed into his nostrils the breath of life' (Genesis 2:7), man became a living thing. It was the Trinity at work, led by Elohim, or God, the strong Creator, who spoke all into existence; Jesus, who holds all things together; and the Holy Spirit, the giver of life. It's the same God, but different functions, or different roles."

Relational God

Seeing that I had the boys' attention, I continued: "We learn that Jesus was in the beginning with God, and everything was made through Him. After God had created all things, He rested and enjoyed everything He had created, especially man.

"Since the beginning, God has showed His desire to have a relationship with man. He had a personal relationship and fellowship with Adam and Eve in the Garden of Eden. He enjoyed good communication with them and favored them. He was their light, but when they disobeyed, darkness entered their lives. Sin scattered their lives; dirty sin caused God to no longer dwell with them. Sin severed the unity and direct friendship they had enjoyed with the creator God.

"Right after Adam and Eve's disobedience, blessings and curses were spoken into their lives. Among other things, they had to learn how to till and keep the land.

"Over time, the people on the earth increased in number. Sin, however, entered their minds and hearts and reigned supreme. They did evil in God's sight, to the point that God was disappointed He had ever made man. Eventually He was fed up and decided to destroy all He had created because of their disobedience and great sin."

God Finds Noah

The account of Noah was next in my storytelling, so I went on: "God was ready to destroy creation, but one man found favor in God's sight, a man named Noah. Because of Noah, creation was given one more chance to live.

"Again God showed us His relational side by communicating to Noah the things to come, instructing him to be ready and to start building an ark. In obedience to God's command, Noah built the ark.

"When the rains came upon the earth, only eight people were spared: Noah and his wife, and their three sons and their wives. Through them, a new generation of human life would burst forth upon the newly renovated land. After they disembarked from the ark, Noah's sons and their wives started to reproduce and fill the earth, as commanded by the Creator. They multiplied still more and became numerous, and through them the nations of the earth were established. But once again sin reigned in the hearts of man.

"Ham, one of Noah's sons and the father of Canaan, sinned against his father. As a result, curses were spoken into his life and his descendants' lives. Ham became the father of the people of Sodom and Gomorrah.

"After that, God was not manifested to His people until the days of Abram. Abram lived in a country with parents and family who worshiped idols and foreign gods. God, however, called him and developed a friendship with him. Soon Abram left his family to go to a land that God would show Him. God eventually changed his name from Abram to Abraham and instructed him to leave the house of his father, named Terah, and settle in the land of Canaan, a land already established but promised to Abraham and his descendants.

"Abraham found favor with the Lord God. God even called him 'friend.' He promised to give Abraham a son and make him the father of a multitude. Abraham, the father of faith, did indeed have a son in his old age, Isaac.

"Isaac, when grown, had twin boys, Esau and Jacob. Jacob, although the younger, was the one in line to rule God's people. Over the years, Jacob developed a friendship with God, and in turn, he directed his children to the Lord God. He taught them about the promises God had given his father Isaac and his grandfather Abraham, and he taught them to hold on to their faith and maintain friendship with the living God.

"The twelve tribes of Israel were descendants of the family of Jacob. Before that, however, Jacob had an encounter with the Angel of the Lord, not knowing it was God whom he wrestled. Jacob prevailed, and the Lord blessed him and gave him a new name: Israel, meaning 'one who prevails with God.'

"As the twelve tribes grew in number, there came a famine in the land where they were living, the land of Canaan, and the sons of Jacob had to turn to the country of Egypt for food. Unknown to them, one of their own was second in command in that country: Joseph, one of Jacob's sons, who had been sold by his brothers as a slave to the Ishmaelites for twenty shekels of silver (Genesis 37:28). These Ishmaelites took Joseph to Egypt.

"The Bible tells us that God was with Joseph and gave him favor with people and blessed him in all that he did. After a series of events, Joseph brought all of Jacob's family to Egypt, where the twelve tribes grew in number. Time passed, Joseph died, and after many years, there was a new ruler in the land of Egypt, a king who had not known Joseph. Because the Israelites, who were Jacob's family and God's people, were so numerous, the king of Egypt feared them and decided to work them as slaves. As a result, they were oppressed and forced into bondage.

"This is what the king of Egypt said to his people: 'Look, the people of the children of Israel are more and mightier than we; come, let us deal shrewdly with them, lest they multiply, and it happen, in the event of war, that they also join our enemies and fight against us, and so go up out of the land' (Exodus 1:8–10). Then the king decided to kill all newborn males in an effort to stop the Israelites from increasing in number.

The suffering of the Israelites was heavy on their shoulders, so much so that the children of Israel had no other option but to turn to the Lord God. The Bible tells us, 'Their cry came up to God because of the bondage. So God heard their groaning, and God remembered His covenant with Abraham, with Isaac, and with Jacob. And God looked upon the children of Israel, and God acknowledged them' (Exodus 2:23–25).

7

"The love of God, the faithfulness of God, was demonstrated in the lives of His people. There was a child to be born in the midst of the people's affliction. Yet once more, the Lord God showed His friendship with His creation."

CHAPTER 2

Take Your Sandals Off Your Feet

Seeing Tommy and his friend so enthusiastic and anxious to learn, I continued speaking and said, "Let me share with you a story of freedom through a faithful servant who brought God's people to the place where they belonged. It is the story of a man named Moses, and it starts when he is but a baby.

"As the enemy neared the house where the baby lived with his parents, there was a loud voice within of one person speaking to another, saying, 'Hurry! We need to save the life of this little one from the hands of the enemy who has gone out killing all newborn babies.' Running from their home to the assigned place, they spotted the perfect basket (cradle) and the perfect person and the perfect place for this newborn baby to survive his oppressors. They gently placed the baby in the basket and set it upon the waters of the Nile River.

"The child was found and taken into the royal residence—the palace. What a divine setup it was when Pharaoh's daughter took the Hebrew baby as her own son, naming him Moses. The boy grew up as a prince, right from the start of his adventurous and appointed life. His life was predestined by the maker of the universe, by the one who saves life, the one who gives life—the great I AM.

"Moses grew up as one of the palace's own. He looked, smelled, and talked like one of them. His exterior resembled their appearance. He was part of an earthly kingdom that perishes with time, a kingdom that lasts only for as long as one is alive, then dies and flies away.

"His interior, however, was built with purpose. His interior was that of a mighty warrior, built and enabled for greatness. His divine calling was to deliver a tribe that, because of a famine in the land, had ended up in a foreign country, a country that enslaved every one of them, making their lives bitter with cruel bondage.

"In the palace where he was raised, Moses had everything he needed: position, wealth, recognition, and all provision. He had it all, lacking nothing, but in his heart he was lacking everything. I believe he felt incomplete. It was a feeling that he did not comprehend or know how to interpret, a feeling of impending greatness and accomplishment. He was a visionary, whose heart and mind were being directed by a power he did not yet understand. Like every young adult, he was full of big dreams and aspirations, not realizing that everything in life requires a price to be paid. Moses had a lot of maturing to do in his personal agenda.

"One day Moses saw one of his people being maltreated by an Egyptian soldier. He took authority into his own hands to defend the Hebrew slave and beat the Egyptian to death.

Pharaoh heard about it and wanted to punish Moses, so Moses fled Egypt in fear for his life."

The Escape

The boys' eyes were focused on me, never leaving my face as I continued the exciting story.

"It was a long and difficult journey through the desert. Moses faced a situation that he had probably never imagined he would face. After years of sleeping on a comfortable, expensive bed in the palace, he found himself sleeping outdoors in the sand—not by choice, but by circumstances brought on through the choices he made. Unlike the palace, the desert was neither accommodating nor secure, but it was now his home.

"By day, Moses suffered from a hot, radiant sun that made him thirst and sweat. Oppressive humidity and blistering sandstorms were now a part of his life. By night, Moses endured coldness and the eerie sounds of creeping things, too many to mention.

"After many days in the desert, Moses arrived at a place where he could find rest and obtain water, a place with green vegetation and food for his empty stomach. He found himself in the middle of a God-fearing family that served the Lord. There, in that land, he worked as a shepherd tending sheep. He eventually married and had children. For forty years, Moses was a foreigner in a foreign land, but he had a dream, a dream to be great, to be noticed, and he also had a heart for his community, his country, and his people.

"While still in Egypt, Moses had risked everything for the sake of his people. Without direction or power, he took it upon himself to do what seemed right in his own eyes; however, his decisions were not powered by a higher authority. The first time he departed Egypt, he left by the backdoor of obscurity, running for his life. However, when he left the second and final time, it was with divine empowerment, faith, wisdom, and determination as he headed for a place already prepared by God Almighty.

"Moses was called to deliver God's people out of the hand of the oppressor. For forty years after he fled Egypt, however, his guilt stopped him from moving forward to discover His true identity, an identity that he had lost when he fled to save his life. On the inside, he knew he was made for greatness, but on the outside, he was a humble shepherd wearing heavy sandals that were dirty from stepping on dirt, dead bugs, and animal droppings of all kinds. His inner sandals, his spiritual ones, were similarly dirtied with shame, guilt, sin, and murder."

The Burning Bush

The enemy had a vast array of guilt to work with in an attempt to prevent Moses from going to the great mountain to meet with God and discover his true identity. One day, however, he overcame all odds and went to the mountaintop—the mountain of God. It was the start of a great journey. The mountain of God had always been in his sight and on his mind, but he had always been too ashamed to climb it. Finally, however, he defeated all fear, conquered his shame, and ascended the mountain. The Bible, in the book of Exodus 3:1–12, tells us the story:

> Moses was tending the flock of Jethro his father-in-law, the priest of Midian. And he led the flock to the back of the desert, and came to Horeb, the mountain of God. And the Angel of the Lord appeared to him in a flame of fire from

the midst of a bush. So he looked, and behold, the bush was burning with fire, but the bush was not consumed. Then Moses said, "I will now turn aside and see this great sight, why the bush does not burn."

So when the LORD saw that he turned aside to look, God called to him from the midst of the bush and said, "Moses, Moses!"

And he said, "Here I am."

Then He said, "Do not draw near this place. Take your sandals off your feet, for the place where you stand is holy ground." Moreover He said, "I am the God of your father—the God of Abraham, the God of Isaac, and the God of Jacob." And Moses hid his face, for he was afraid to look upon God.

And the LORD said: "I have surely seen the oppression of My people who are in Egypt, and have heard their cry because of their taskmasters, for I know their sorrows. So I have come down to deliver them out of the hand of the Egyptians, and to bring them up from that land to a good and large land, to a land flowing with milk and honey. . . . Now therefore, behold, the cry of the children of Israel has come to Me, and I have also seen the oppression with which the Egyptians oppress them. Come now, therefore, and I will send you to Pharaoh that you may bring My people, the children of Israel, out of Egypt."

But Moses said to God, "Who am I that I should go to Pharaoh, and that I should bring the children of Israel out of Egypt?"

So He said, "I will certainly be with you. And this shall be a sign to you that I have sent you: When you have brought the people out of Egypt, you shall serve God on this mountain."

What do we learn from this teaching? We learn that Moses was hungry to meet God. He surrendered completely to Him, met with Him, served Him, and followed His guidance accordingly. Moses understood God, and He respected Him and embraced His orders.

Tommy and his friend Learned so much from my storytelling, however the new teachings coming up I have not shared with them yet. I felt they were too young to understand. My prayer is that when they are ready to learn and understand, they would apply them.

CHAPTER 3

Holy Ground

"Take your sandals off your feet, for the place where you stand *is* holy ground."

—Exodus.3:5

When God revealed this passage to me, He showed me that Moses needed to be purified because, remember, he was a sinner, a murderer. God was basically saying, "Moses, if you are going to serve Me, you need to get rid of all old things. You need to repent and be forgiven. You need to be renewed, to be born again—you need a new life. You need to prepare yourself, Moses, because you are entering the divine presence of God."

The Shekinah glory of God is the place of mysterious sanctity where He manifests Himself. If we come before Him acceptably, approaching Him with reverence, submission, and respect. I believe that Moses' taking his shoes off was a representation of his respect and total submission to the Lord God. When we draw near to Him, it should be with solemn pause and preparation, with a humble, teachable, open-minded attitude ready to receive revelation, orders, favor, and guidance. The true God was being revealed to Moses, the God of his forefathers whom he longed to know.

It was not that the place where Moses was standing was holy. Rather, it was the presence of the holy God that made it holy. Moses responded by not only removing his shoes, but also hiding his face, a sign that he understood he was in the presence of the Shekinah glory of God. Moses was conscious of his own sinfulness and unworthiness. He was so aware of God's holiness that he was afraid to look at Him face-to-face. The splendor was so great that Moses, in his sinful nature, did not dare to look directly upon the glory of God. He was supported by his flesh alone, not yet overshadowed with the Spirit of the most high God.

The ground where Moses stood was rendered sacred by the presence of God Almighty, who is the very essence of holiness. In our day, the phrase *holy ground* refers to not only a place of worship or a place of meeting, but also a place of divine order and service. Not only is God teaching us that we should enter the place set apart for divine worship with reverence in our hearts, but He is also calling us to live our daily lives as if we are always in His presence, which we are. We need to always walk with a pure heart and "without our sandals," because if we proclaim, teach, preach, pray, live, and share the Word of God, then we are always standing on holy ground, for wherever the Lord is constitutes holy ground.

Holy Ground

Holy ground is not a physical place, but a spiritual one. When the Lord God commanded Moses to take his sandals off because he was standing on holy ground, He was not referring to a twelve-by-twelve piece of real state. He was referring to a spiritual state.

The place where Moses was standing was holy! What place? The spiritual condition he had finally come to. He had arrived at a place in his personal growth where God could work though him. Moses on those 40 years of learning had grown and matured enough to surrender completely to the Lord God. He was now at the place of reception, ready to listen and take orders. He was mature and ready to serve the Lord God in all He commanded.

There are many people today who are stepping on holy ground but don't want to take their sandals off their feet. For example, many males wear not one but two earrings. I say "males" because real men stay away from that; as someone has said, only sissies and girls wear earrings. If that describes you, I'm not judging you, but Jesus did say that a tree is known by its fruit. I'm not stupid, and though I am neither a judge nor a fruit inspector, I can identify a tree in front of me by what it looks like and by the fruit it bears. As 1 Corinthians 2:15 says, "But he who is spiritual judges all things, yet he himself is rightly judged by no one."

I don't know about you, but if I am called to be a light, then I want to be one; I want to shine for the Lord. People in the world often call Christians hypocrites, and that is the reason why: because we often say one thing but act the opposite. Come on—let's be doers of the Word, not hearers only. The Bible clearly teaches that everyone who proclaims the name of the Lord should stay away from iniquity, or sin (2 Timothy 2:19).

At the Last Supper, Jesus was with His disciples, the ones He had called to be witnesses of the kingdom of God. Although they were His followers, He began to wash their feet, saying, "He who is bathed needs only to wash his feet, but is completely clean; and you are clean, but not all of you" (John 13:10). Notice the words "not all of you." When Jesus said this at the Last Supper, Judas, His betrayer, was present. Peter, who had denied Him three times, was also there. Thomas, the one who had doubted, was present as well. Here we learn that the Twelve were not only stepping onto holy ground but were also in the presence of the Holy One. They were followers of Jesus, but not all of them were righteous. Some had followed Him just to follow, pursuing possessions, material gain, financial gain, or popularity. In the case of Judas, he was the treasurer, the one who carried the money box. He was into money and sold what was not his.

Not all are clean, just the few who understand that to serve God is to know Him. Are you stepping onto holy ground? How is the condition of your heart? Are you already serving on holy ground? How is the condition of your heart? Are you clean?

Faithful Servant

I learned long ago why a few faithful servants of the Lord can speak the truth without sugarcoating it, and that is because they can't be fired! But seriously, it is because they have met God and He has sent them, just like He sent Moses and others to free His people, to proclaim the good news, to tell the truth as it is written.

It is so fascinating when I meet a true follower and servant of God. I can feel his pure heart, and the Spirit of the Lord gives me assurance that the person is a true disciple of the Lord. You can pick out a servant of the Lord from miles away. I believe that when Pharaoh met Moses, he could tell that he was for real and that the power of the Lord was with him. Obviously, he saw the miracles Moses performed with the rod of God, but he also saw the person Moses had become: a bold, sincere, faithful man who was determined to do what he was commanded to do.

In the following pages of this book, you will learn about people who were directly commanded by the Lord God to "take their sandals off." I invite you to open your heart and mind to grasp the revelation and teaching that will come your way. I pray your life will be touched and transformed in Jesus' name. Amen!

CHAPTER 4

A Daily Walk in His Presence

Before you continue reading, I invite you to "take your sandals off your feet" before the Lord God, not physically, but spiritually. Take a few minutes to meditate on that command. Now let's enter into His presence and pray:

Father in heaven, we thank You for permitting us to come into Your presence. We come before You, repenting of all our sins, transgressions, and disobedience. We offer our bodies as a living sacrifice, and we ask you to cleanse our bodies, purify our hearts, and renew our minds. Help us to resist the temptations of this world. Guide us and keep us under Your wings, and protect us from the evil one and his angels. Empower us to live holy in all areas of our lives. Let the pages of this book lead us and make us understand You in the simplest and easiest way possible. In Jesus' name we pray. Amen.

In our walk with God, He has promised to always be with us. Those words are like a sweet melody ringing in our ears in everything we do—our coming in and our going out, at all times.

In all the steps we take and in every breath we draw, we have the assurance that He will never leave us.

The Bible is the living Word of God, and it is powerful and life-changing. The promises of the written Word of God are clearly expressed in 2 Timothy 3:16, where we learn that, "All Scripture is inspired by God and is useful to teach us what is true and to make us realize what is wrong in our lives. It corrects us when we are wrong and teaches us to do what is right" (NLT). With this promise of God in hand, we can be assured that what we learn in the Bible comes directly from God Himself.

In writing the Bible, God used regular people—people like you and me, people who desired to know and serve Him with everything they had. This love story from God begins in the book of Genesis, where we see that He made everything in love.

In the Old Testament, we learn about God's greatness and power. When Jesus appears in the Old Testament, he is referred to as "the Angel of the LORD." In the New Testament, He is "the Spirit of the Lord." Through Moses in the Old Testament, God revealed His mysteries; through Jesus in the New Testament, He demonstrates His love and friendship with us.

In the New Testament, we experience God's love through relationship. When God came to live with us in the person of Jesus Christ, He showed us His love and kindness and His faithfulness to us. He came to show us the way, the truth, and the life.

In the book of John, we learn that, "In the beginning was the Word, and the Word was with God, and the Word was God" (John 1:1). The chapter goes on to say that everything was made through the Word. The Word here is referring to Jesus. In other words, everything in creation was made through Jesus and for

Jesus. Continuing in John, we learn that the Word became human and lived among us. That speaks of Jesus, the main character of the Bible from beginning to end, from cover to cover. The Bible is a book all about Him, His work, His life, His teachings, and His promises for us to follow, obey, and live by.

In the Bible are many promises to receive and instructions to live by. Here are just a few:

To Moses, God promised, "I will certainly be with you" (Exodus 3:12).

Psalm 119:105 tells us that His Word is a lamp to our feet and a light to our path.

Micah 6:8 instructs us: "He has shown you, O man, what is good; and what does the Lord require of you but to do justly, to love mercy, and to walk humbly with your God?"

Galatians 5:16 encourages us to "Walk in the Spirit, and you shall not fulfill the lust of the flesh."

John 4:24 reminds us, "God is Spirit, and those who worship Him must worship in spirit and truth."

First John 4:4 proclaims, "He who is in you is greater than he who is in the world."

But in my opinion, the greatest promise of all is found in John 14:23, when Jesus said, "If anyone loves Me, he will keep My word; and My Father will love him, and We will come to him and make Our home with him." In this promise, God is again teaching relationship. God is a God of *relationship*, not *religion-ship*.

"If anyone loves Me" is an open invitation to all. It doesn't matter who you are—He is inviting anyone and everyone.

When Jesus said, "My Father will love him," we see that God rewards obedience; as He said in the Old Testament, obedience is better than sacrifice.

"We will come to him" is such an awesome promise. Once we remove the sandals from our feet and walk in love, obedience, and truth to Him and in the service of others, our reward is reserved.

The last part of the verse, "and make Our home with him," is a direct promise from God. God the Father will favor anyone who is all in for Him. If this describes you, then God the Father and God the Son will come and reside with you. They will live in you, a promise that means if you live in harmony and love with your Creator, He will not leave you or forsake you. He will always be there with you.

Another great promise is found in Matthew 28:20, when Jesus said, "I am with you always, even to the end of the age." Jesus made this promise after His resurrection, but before His ascension into heaven when all power and authority were given to Him on earth as it is in heaven. Therefore, we have no reason to fear, but rather, we can walk boldly and humbly hand in hand with the resurrected King.

We do this through the Spirit, who is with us at all times. When Jesus promised not to leave us alone, He also promised to send the Helper, the Comforter, the Spirit of truth. He is with us in every step we take, every decision we make, and all that we do. He is there just like the wind, invisible yet very present. It is through the third person of the Trinity, the Holy Spirit, that we can walk holy. He empowers us, directs us to resist the devil, and enables us to live righteously in His forever presence.

Did you know that God gave the same promise to His children, the Israelites, back in the days of Isaiah, a servant of the Lord who walked the walk? God said to them, "Fear not, for I have redeemed you; I have called you by your name; you are Mine" (Isaiah 43:1). Here we learn again that God is a relational God, a relational God who speaks directly to His people as their creator. Because of that, God has a special and unique claim upon all of us. When we ignore or reject God as Father, Creator, and Lord, we fail in the most basic obligation we have to Him: to love and obey Him.

Let's break down Isaiah 43:1 like we did with John 14:23. First is "Fear not." Not only is this a direct command, but it also implies a promise. Our battle is not one of flesh and blood, but it is a spiritual war, and spiritual wars are fought in the Spirit. It is God Himself who fights our spiritual battles. As long as we are connected to Him and wearing the full armor that He provides, we can step forth in boldness, knowing that He is always there to protect us.

"For I have redeemed you" comes next. We have an obligation to God, not only as our creator, but also as our redeemer. He is the one who paid the ultimate price for all humanity. He set us free and gave us the opportunity to be saved if we will just come to Him. As He said, "If the Son makes you free, you shall be free indeed" (John 8:36). When God calls Himself our redeemer, it looks to the price that has been paid for our salvation.

"I have called you by your name; You are Mine" shows that God knows you personally. He knows your name, and you are His. He even knows the number of hairs on your head. God twice owns His children: He has right of ownership both as Creator and as Redeemer. Knowing we belong to the Lord is a wonderful promise that empowers us not to walk in fear. Like the hen that gathers her chicks under her wings, we can be sure that He holds us, protects us, guards us, and cares for us (Matthew 23:37). We know that He would not have created, redeemed, and called us unless He intended to guide us, equip us, and finish His work in us. How can we be afraid when we know that God is on our side and grants us favor?

Let's read a bit more in Isaiah 43:

> When you pass through the waters, I will be with you; and through the rivers, they shall not overflow you. When you walk through the fire, you shall not be burned, nor shall the flame scorch you. For I am the LORD your God, the Holy One of Israel, your Savior; I gave Egypt for your ransom, Ethiopia and Seba in your place. Since you were precious in My sight, you have been honored, and I have loved you; therefore I will give men for you, and people for your life. Fear not, for I am with you; I will bring your descendants from the east, and gather you from the west; I will say to the north, "Give them up!" and to the south, "Do not keep them back!" Bring My sons from afar, and My daughters from the ends of the earth; everyone who is called by My name, whom I have created for My glory; I have formed him, yes, I have made him." (verses 2–7)

Here in this passage, the Lord makes His love for us personal. Once you develop a friendship with the Lord, you soon develop a holy walk. You know that His presence is always with you, and once that happens, your life becomes different. You are now a transformed being. You live by faith, and you have spiritual wisdom. You have a new life, and because of that new life, you now see through the eyes of Jesus. You love through the heart of the Lord, speak through the mouth of Jesus, and think through His mind. As you walk in His footsteps, you are able to hear His voice and obey it. You learn to depend on Him in all areas of your life, finances, friendships, family, etc. You mature to a level of leadership and ownership where you can now execute His plans and apply all that He has taught you to your everyday life.

I have been walking a holy life (not perfect, but holy) for about five years. I have learned to depend on God 100 percent. I have chosen to listen to positive Christian music and to stay away from TV for more than ten years now. Every day I'm praising and worshiping the Lord in my house and out of it, and on my way to work, at work, and on my way back home, all by choice. God has given me the ability to hear His voice. As Jesus says, "My sheep hear my voice" (John 10:27).

One day I was driving while listening to worship music on the radio when all of a sudden I heard the voice of God asking me, "What is it that you want?" When I heard those words, it reminded me that we all ask God for things. We say, "God, I want this . . . I want that." We learn early to ask for things, don't we?

When God asked me that question, I seemed to enter directly into His presence for an entire minute. Immediately I thought about what I wanted. In that one minute, I felt as if I were one-on-one in the Spirit with God. I looked at my life, searching for what I wanted, but I did not find a thing. I was overwhelmed in His presence, realizing that my life had been so joyful and peaceful for so many years that I could not find a thing to ask for.

Nothing came to my mind—I felt complete. I could not say a thing, so I said nothing. I remained quiet, nothing coming out of my mouth. A minute later, I came back to the flesh and answered Him, saying, "God, can I get back to You on that one?" Even then, I could not find a thing to ask Him for.

As I later meditated on the experience, I realized that with God I had it all. With Him I was complete. I had peace of mind, joy in my heart, a beautiful family, and ample provision. I had everything I needed and could not identify one single thing I lacked. I needed only Jesus, and with Him I was complete.

No, I do not own a 911 Porsche Turbo, a mansion, or a yacht. Do I want them? Maybe, but I don't need them. They are not important to me—they are not my priorities. What I want more than anything else is a holy walk with God. Enoch walked with God, and God took him to heaven. Elijah too walked with God, and he also was transported to heaven. Moses walked with God, and from the transfiguration we learn that he is in eternity with God the Father. Throughout the ages, many others have walked a holy walk and enjoyed God's protection, provision, and blessing in their lives here on earth. How about you? How is your walk in His presence?

In closing this chapter, let me share a passage from Exodus. I believe it will show you the importance of having a holy walk in the presence of God:

> Behold, I send an Angel before you to keep you in the way
> and to bring you into the place which I have prepared. Beware
> of Him and obey His voice; do not provoke Him, for He will
> not pardon your transgressions; for My name is in Him. But

if you indeed obey His voice and do all that I speak, then I will be an enemy to your enemies and an adversary to your adversaries. . . .

So you shall serve the LORD your God, and He will bless your bread and your water. And I will take sickness away from the midst of you.

Exodus 23:20–22, 25

CHAPTER 5

The Mysteries Revealed

Once you are purified of your worldly walk, God will lead you by His Spirit through His valley and onto holy ground. There you will be taught and given instructions and resources to do His will. There in the unholy world, He will use you mightily, His hand and Spirit upon you. You will be given a sword, the sword of the Spirit. It's similar to receiving a heart transplant, but now your heart will be empowered by the ultimate and most immaculate force—the Spirit of the most high God. He will direct your path, give you the words to say, and guide you all the steps of your way.

God's glory manifests when we obediently do His will. He is glorified every time we do anything in His name. His name is indeed great, and a day will come when every knee will bow to Him. He is the great I AM.

From the foundation of time, God has revealed all mysteries through His chosen ones, especially through God the Son, starting with His birth through a virgin mother. His baptism was a pivotal point, something that we all must emulate in order to see and understand the kingdom of God.

The Transfiguration

In the transfiguration, God was teaching and declaring to believers that Jesus was His Son and He was well pleased with Him.

What a magnificent scene it was! Jesus took three of His disciples to witness this exuberant, brilliant, and luminous mystery of the kingdom of God. The transfiguration is one of six major mysteries in the gospel narrative of the life of our Lord Jesus Christ, the others being His birth, baptism, crucifixion, resurrection, and ascension. In this scene, Jesus was transfigured before His small group composed of Peter, James, and John, His three chosen ones.

In the book of Matthew we learn that, "His face shone as the sun, and His garments became as white as light. At that point, the prophets Elijah and Moses appeared, and Jesus began to talk to them. The witnesses also heard the voice of God saying, 'This is My beloved Son, in whom I am well pleased. Hear Him!'" (Matthew 17:2-5).

Not Moses, not Elijah, but Jesus was being identified by God the Father as His only begotten Son. In this way, the disciples could comprehend that there was only one Savior, one way to God the Father in heaven, and that was through Jesus, the Savior of the whole world.

Just as Moses and Elijah began to depart from that marvelous scene, Peter reacted in the flesh and said, "Rabbi, it is good for us to be here; and let us make three tabernacles: one for You, one for Moses, and one for Elijah." (Luke 2:5). That was not what God was teaching them. Rather, He was teaching about God's glory and the kingdom of God on earth, as well as the way it is in heaven. God was teaching that the whole world revolves around Jesus and no one else. That is why the voice of God added, "Listen to Him," because in Him are truth and joy, in Him were all things created, and in Him lay all the Law and the Prophets.

I once heard a preacher say that in the transfiguration, Moses represented the Law, and Elijah represented the Prophets. He then asked his congregation, "What did Jesus represent?" He provided the answer by saying, "He was representing you and me." I would add that Jesus represents God first and then unites us to Him. He is the bridge between God and man.

CHAPTER 6

Born Again

That day when so many people were baptized, "It came to pass that Jesus also was baptized; and while He prayed, the heaven was opened. And the Holy Spirit descended in bodily form like a dove upon Him, and a voice came from heaven which said, 'You are My beloved Son; in You I am well pleased'" (Luke 3:21–22).

God makes baptism very personal. When Jesus was water baptized, God said from heaven, "You are my beloved Son; in You I am well pleased" (verse 22).

God indeed spoke those words to Jesus, but we too are His sons and daughters. Therefore, when we are water baptized, He rejoices and identifies us as His sons and daughters. We become His elect children. This is seen in the story of Mary Magdalene's encounter with Jesus after His resurrection.

When Mary saw Him, Jesus said to her, "Don't cling to me . . . for I haven't yet ascended to the Father. But go find my *brothers* and tell them, 'I am ascending to my Father and your Father, to my God and your God'" (John 20:17 NLT, emphasis added). It cannot be any clearer than that: "Tell my brothers that

I'm going back to my Father and your Father; I'm going back to my God and your God."

Can We Lose Sonship?

You may be wondering whether we can lose our sonship with God after we are born again and become His son or daughter. The answer is no. We cannot lose sonship after we are born again. We may stray and run away from our home and our heavenly Father, losing His protection, blessing, and provision, but we don't lose sonship. This is illustrated clearly in the well-known parable of the prodigal son.

The prodigal son asked for his inheritance and decided to call his own shots; he wanted to live the way of the world in his own way. When he had finally spent all his treasure, he found himself desolate, living a miserable life of want and lack. Although he was in that situation as a result of his own actions and choices, he was still his father's son. His father was still his father.

One day the young man came to his senses and returned to his father's house, where there was plenty. What did the father do upon his son's return? Did he reject him? Did he condemn him? Did he tell him he was no longer his son? No, he did none of those things. Instead, he welcomed him home, hugged him tightly, saw that he was bathed and clothed, and then threw a huge banquet for him. His father received back to himself a son who had been lost, who was dead but had come alive.

The prodigal son never lost his position of sonship, even when he was living far from his father's home. The same holds true for us if we decide to go the same route. We will not lose sonship, but we will lose the protection, provision, and all that comes when we live within our Father's boundaries. When we refuse to live according to His rules, we are on our own. On our own, we will certainly get lost, perhaps even heading to the lake of fire. On his own, the prodigal son was hopelessly lost, and as a son or daughter of God, you too will be lost if you go your own way.

Although the prodigal son was physically absent from his father, his father was still his father, and the prodigal was still his son. He was lost, but he was still his father's son. His father could not force him to return home. The prodigal had to recognize that he had done wrong, ask for forgiveness, and then allow himself to be made whole. Similarly, we serve a forgiving God, a graceful heavenly Father who does not abandon us but waits for us to make a U-turn and run into His open arms.

Judas Iscariot was one of Jesus' disciples, but Judas allowed his own desires to overtake him and did not repent and ask for forgiveness. He was overtaken by evil and disobeyed and sinned. Tragically, he ended up taking his own life. As the Scriptures remind us, the wages of sin is death.

Best of Both Worlds

The world wields tremendous influence on the things we want. The Word of God, however, teaches us the way, the truth, and the life we ought to be living. If we study both, we will discover a big difference between the two.

The world offers pleasures of all kind, pleasures that last for only brief periods of time. Some of these pleasures leave marks on the soul and bring disgrace. The world offers fun, but it's the kind of fun that leaves us empty, unhappy, and unfulfilled. The kingdom of God, however, offers peace of mind, joy, and blessing, intangible rewards of great fulfillment.

There is a song called "The Best of Both Worlds." If you are a true disciple of Christ, then that is not for you. You are in either one world or the other, but you cannot live in both. How can you live worldly and godly at the same time? Proverbs 10:22 reminds us, " The blessing of the LORD makes one rich, and He adds no sorrow with it." Proverbs 11:30 adds, "The fruit of the righteous is a tree of life, and he who wins souls is wise."

After the prodigal son lost all his belongings, he could go no other way but up—and he got up. Leaving behind his disobedience, shame, pride, and fear, he decided to return to his blessed life, a life full of provision and love. But most importantly, he went home to a life of freedom, freedom to walk and do all he was allowed to do in his father's mansion.

Many of us preach on the prodigal son and emphasize the love and forgiveness shown when he returned home. We often end the story right there, but we really shouldn't. The story of the prodigal son continues, and in actuality, it gets even better. What did the prodigal son do after he was welcomed home and forgiven? He obeyed! He did not sin again, but became a new person. He was renewed, born again, and continued to walk in obedience to his father's rules.

New Life

For many people, the fear of death is great. One of the reasons is that they know they have disobeyed God's statutes, and deep in their souls, they know that at Judgment Day they will reap what they have planted. Remember, if you have denied the Lord, He will deny you as well. For many, dying is loss; for others, dying is gain. For many, dying is the end; for others, dying is only the beginning.

Someone once said, "When you are born once, you die twice; but when you are born twice, you die once!" When you are born physically but never reborn in Christ, your flesh eventually dies, and you also die spiritually by not receiving eternal life. When you are born physically but then are reborn and enter God's kingdom, your flesh still dies one day, but you continue to live everlasting life in Jesus.

This is what 1 Thessalonians 5:5–10 tell us about our future destination:

> You are all sons of light and sons of the day. We are not of the night nor of darkness. Therefore let us not sleep, as others do, but let us watch and be sober. For those who sleep, sleep at night, and those who get drunk are drunk at night. But let us who are of the day be sober, putting on the breastplate of faith and love, and as a helmet the hope of salvation. For God did not appoint us to wrath, but to obtain salvation through our Lord Jesus Christ, who died for us, that whether we wake or sleep, we should live together with Him.

Human Nature

Because of our human nature, we cannot comprehend spiritual things. Because of our sinful nature, we can understand only earthly things. Heavenly things are foolishness to the sinful man. Once we are born again, however, we gain understanding of divine things. The story of Nicodemus in the New Testament demonstrates this clearly:

There was a man of the Pharisees named Nicodemus, a ruler of the Jews. This man came to Jesus by night and said to Him, "Rabbi, we know that You are a teacher come from God; for no one can do these signs that You do unless God is with him."

Jesus answered and said to him, "Most assuredly, I say to you, unless one is born again, he cannot see the kingdom of God."

Nicodemus said to Him, "How can a man be born when he is old? Can he enter a second time into his mother's womb and be born?"

Jesus answered, "Most assuredly, I say to you, unless one is born of water and the Spirit, he cannot enter the kingdom of God. That which is born of the flesh is flesh, and that which is born of the Spirit is spirit. Do not marvel that I said to you, 'You must be born again.' The wind blows where it wishes, and you hear the sound of it, but cannot tell where it comes from and where it goes. So is everyone who is born of the Spirit."

Nicodemus answered and said to Him, "How can these things be?"

Jesus answered and said to him, "Are you the teacher of Israel, and do not know these things? Most assuredly, I say to you, We speak what We know and testify what We have seen, and you do not receive Our witness. If I have told you earthly things and you do not believe, how will you believe if I tell you heavenly things?"

John 3:1–12

We cannot understand creation until we understand the Creator. Before my baptism, I was dead spiritually. I could not understand anything of a spiritual nature until I was born again and received new life in Christ.

New Spiritual Birth

Peter was one of the greatest visionaries ever known to man. He had a big heart that was full of love for the Lord. Little by little, the Spirit of God revealed to him God's kingdom. Numerous times in the Gospels, Jesus had to correct or even rebuke Peter. For example, on one occasion, Peter protested Jesus' words about His future, and Jesus replied, "Get behind me, Satan!" This same Peter walked on water for a split second but then sank. When he saw Moses, Elijah, and Jesus together in the transfiguration, he suggested that three tents be built for them. He had a great heart full of compassion, but he did not yet understand heavenly things.

When the soldiers came to arrest Jesus, Peter took his sword and cut off the ear of one of the soldiers. (I do not believe Peter was aiming at the person's ear, but accidentally got it.) There he was—defending His teacher. Jesus, of course, rebuked Peter, saying, "Put your sword in its place, for all who take the sword will perish by the sword. Or do you think that I cannot now pray to My Father, and He will provide Me with more than twelve legions of angels? How then could the Scriptures be fulfilled, that it must happen thus?" (Matthew 26:52–54).

Now if you think about it, Peter did all he was capable of, and perhaps the only thing he was able to do. However, Peter was acting in the flesh. He did not yet understand spiritual things and would not until his reencounter with the Lord Jesus. He did all things in accordance with his human nature. This same Peter who loved the Lord, who proclaimed to Him that he would never leave Him, in the end did exactly what Jesus told him he would do, and that was to deny Him three times. Peter desperately needed a new birth—a rebirth. He needed to be transformed, to be born again, in order to understand the kingdom of God as Jesus taught it.

After Jesus' resurrection, this same Peter reencountered the Lord in an entirely new way. Jesus blew His Spirit on Peter, and his mind was opened to understand the Scriptures and the mysteries of the kingdom of God (John 20:22; Luke 24:45). Once Peter received forgiveness from the Lord and the promise of the Holy Spirit, his life was forever transformed. Now he had the courage to boldly proclaim the gospel because he finally understood the way, the truth, and the life of our divine Redeemer.

It is certain that Peter was being prepared during those three years he walked with Jesus. At the time, he did not fully grasp the spiritual concept of taking his sandals off his feet. Even though Jesus physically washed Peter's feet, he did not understand that Jesus was preparing him for the coming of the Comforter. When Jesus indicated His intention of washing Peter's feet, Peter responded, "Lord, not my feet only, but also my hands and my head!" (John 13:9). Peter wanted Jesus to wash all of his body because he knew who Jesus was, and he wanted to be with the

Lord and be a part of Him wherever He went. Peter understood that Jesus was the Messiah, the Christ, the Son of God—the one he needed to follow, abide with, and serve on a holy walk in His everlasting presence.

Acts 1:8 records the coming of the Comforter to the disciples. The Holy Spirit came to stay with us, lead us, prepare us, convict us, comfort us, transform us, and empower us.

Turn Your Switch On

It's been over two thousand years since Jesus made His disciples an everlasting promise, a promise that has been available since it was first given, the promise of the Holy Spirit. Jesus said these words in Acts 1:8: "But you shall receive power when the Holy Spirit has come upon you; and you shall be witnesses to Me in Jerusalem, and in all Judea and Samaria, and to the end of the earth." You may be thinking, *Well, that promise was personally given to Jesus' disciples. That was a promise to them back then.* Yes, it was a promise made to the disciples, but it also applies to all those who came after. As soon as you become one of Jesus' disciples, that promise is also yours. All you have to do is receive it in the name of Jesus.

Five years ago, I received that promise of the Holy Spirit for myself. Before I received, it felt like my light switch to God was disconnected. I was spiritually dead, but after I became born again and received the promise of the Holy Spirit, my light switch was turned on. That was the beginning of a powerful reencounter with the Lord God. My wineskin had to be new in order to receive the promise of the Spirit, and I had to take my sandals off in order to walk on holy ground.

Where Are You?

If you look for the Holy Spirit physically, you will not find Him. You can look up, down, and sideways, but He is not there. That's because He dwells within in the hearts of all those who believe. We are His temple and He has made His home with us.

Those who are of the world cannot understand this. As John 14:17 says, "The Spirit of truth, whom the world cannot receive, because it neither sees Him nor knows Him; but you know Him, for He dwells with you and will be in you." Jesus said, "Unless one is born again, he cannot see the kingdom of God" (John 3:3); and then He added, "Unless one is born of water and the Spirit, he cannot enter the kingdom of God" (verse 5).

The prodigal son was lost and headed for destruction until he realized that his ways were not enlightened, but darkened. He found the way home, obeyed his father, and enjoyed a new life and a new beginning—a chance to start over. We have all been there; we all need a redeemer who will take us as we are. Jesus is the one who cleanses, purifies, and makes us new.

CHAPTER 7

Shoe Covers

I did construction work in New York for ten years. The houses there were older than the ones in Georgia, where I live today. If I remember correctly, not often did people ask me to remove my shoes when entering their homes, unless they had brand-new carpet or a freshly mopped floor. Nonetheless, whenever I entered a house, I would take my shoes off, showing respect for the home just as I always do at my house. Most of the homeowners, however, would say, "You are fine. You don't have to take your shoes off." This always made me uncomfortable because my shoes were usually dusty and dirty from the work I had been doing.

Customarily, I removed my shoes before entering a client's home, but several times I went to a house and the floor was such mess that I did not want to do so. I did not want to dirty my socks and carry all that back into my shoes as soon as I put them back on. Interestingly, the customer in this kind of home would sometimes ask, "Would you please remove your shoes?" On one occasion like this, I did remove my shoes, but afterwards my socks were so filthy that I had to remove them immediately and throw them out. After that instance, I learned to cover my shoes with shoe covers. I went to the store to buy some, and there they were—shoe covers. Now, whenever I go into a house, I cover my shoes. It is a great feeling to know that because of my shoe covers, the floor is safe from any dirt that may be on my shoes, and I am safe from any dirt that may be on the floor.

Although this process functions marvelously in the physical, it does not work in the spiritual. We cannot cover up our faults, hang-ups, wrongdoing, and sins. When we come before the Lord, we need to remove our shoes completely. That is what He is asking us to do—to remove our shoes and not cover up any flaws.

In the Garden of Eden, God covered the sinners (Adam and Eve), not the sin. The sin was exposed to the light and taken care of. When people attempt to cover their shoes (sins), they also learn to cover the sins of others. Think about that for a second.

Legalism

I hear many preachers today talking about legalism, or strict conformity to a set of preestablished rules. Some people or organizations take their own understanding of something, subject their people to it, and carry it to an extreme. They demand conformity to their standards.

Sad to say, but in today's society, right and good are out, and unrighteousness is in. Though we have many churches, there is so much of the world in some of them that you do not know where you are. I mean, you are physically in church, but you wonder if you really are. You look around and see people dressed as though they were going to a nightclub, ladies with low- cut blouses and short skirts, and men sporting earrings. We even see men who call themselves pastors who are preaching with earrings on. I mean, what are they doing? I'm not a legalist, but come on!

Think about it. Was God being a legalist when He gave Moses moral rules of conduct in the book of Leviticus? Chapter 19 spells out His requirements in full detail. Was God being a legalist when He commanded, "You shall not make any cuttings in your flesh for the dead, nor tattoo any marks on you" (Leviticus 19:28)? Oh yeah, we are living on the edge, in different times now. Really? Times and seasons change, but the Word of God remains the same. The hearts and behavior of people may change, but not the Word of the Lord. It is forever the same. Yes, we are living in a new day. We cannot deny that, but we must remember that the Word of God was from the beginning—and still is. The Word does not change; it always has been and always will be the same.

What many people do is take the Word on their own terms instead of living out the Word in their lives. In that scenario, the sandals are not fully off the feet; they are merely covered. If you ask some preachers today what they are preaching or doing about any of the important issues that we face—abortion, adultery, homosexuality, divorce, fornication—they respond, "I do not want to offend anyone." If you are a preacher, minister, pastor, or any kind of leader in your church or organization, what are you doing when you say that? You do not want to offend anyone? Are you for real? You are already offending God! You have already denied His Word. You are just covering the sin of others, and you certainly have not yet removed your own sandals. Your shoes are covered, and you are not walking the way God asked you to walk.

Nathan, when he came to unveil David's wrongdoing, refused to cover David's sin. Instead, Nathan told him what God expected and the consequences that would follow David's actions. David was forgiven of his sins, but his possessions would be awarded to others. God did not cover David's sin. In fact, He brought it out into the open and said: "Behold, I will raise up adversity against you from your own house; and I will take your wives before your eyes and give them to your neighbor, and he shall lie with your wives in the sight of this sun. For you did it secretly, but I will do this thing before all Israel, before the sun" (2 Samuel 12:11–12). Here we learn that God does not cover anyone's sin, so why should we? Tell the truth and expose sin.

God was faithful, forgiving, and fair when He judged David's sinful deeds. You see, when we disobey the ways of the Lord, we are the ones who are hurting ourselves. We do the wrong things and suffer the consequences, but then we start blaming God, asking, "Why, God? Why did You allow this to happen to me?" Let me remind you that we all have a free will. God will not stop us from doing things. The Holy Spirit, however, will warn us when we are about to do wrong, but if we have no understanding of the Spirit, those warnings are useless. We need to learn how God works in the Spirit so we can be instructed and led by Him.

Did Moses, when he came back with the tablets and saw the people worshiping a handmade statue cover their sin? No, he executed truth and condemnation and its consequences. He had already given them God's mandate of righteousness, the rules of righteous living. It was the people's choice to either receive it and obey, or deny it and disobey. We all know what happened to all those who wandered in the desert for forty years. They all perished, all denied entrance to the Promised Land because of their wrongdoing and disobedience to the most high God.

Remember, when you cover your shoes—that is, your faults and your filthiness—your sins are still walking with you. When you merely cover your shoes, you have not completely surrendered to God. You think that by covering yours faults or sins, you will be okay. You may be okay in the sight of man, but you are not okay in the sight of God.

The reason you do wrong things is that you do not understand God and ultimately do not know Him. Remember the word of the Lord God when He said, "If anyone loves me, he will keep my word; and My Father will love him, and We will come to him and make Our home with him" (John 14:23).

"The commandments are of the Old Testament," you may protest, but remember that Jesus came to fulfill them—not to hide them or remove them, but to apply them. Without the Old Testament, there would be no New Testament, and vice versa. But rejoice, because He came to rescue the sick and the sinner and bring them to new life.

Therefore, without sin, there is no grace.

Without confusion, there is no understanding.

Without repentance, there is no forgiveness of sin.

Without Jesus, there is no life.

That being said, we all are sinners in the sight of the Lord, and we all have the opportunity to come clean and be renewed. We all need a redeemer—we need Christ in our daily lives.

Captivity as a Result of Disobedience

There is a story in Zechariah 7:8–14 that I would like to share. It reads as follows:

> Then the word of the LORD came to Zechariah, saying, "Thus says the LORD of hosts:
>> 'Execute true justice,
>> Show mercy and compassion
>> Everyone to his brother.
>> Do not oppress the widow or the fatherless,
>> The alien or the poor.
>> Let none of you plan evil in his heart
>> Against his brother.'
>
> "But they refused to heed, shrugged their shoulders, and stopped their ears so that they could not hear. Yes, they made their hearts like flint, refusing to hear the law and the words which the LORD of hosts had sent by His Spirit through the former prophets. Thus great wrath came from the LORD of hosts. Therefore it happened, that just as He proclaimed and they would not hear, so they called out and I would not listen," says the LORD of hosts. "But I scattered them with a whirlwind among all the nations which they had not known. Thus the land became desolate after them, so that no one passed through or returned; for they made the pleasant land desolate."

God wants us clean and purified. He wants us for Himself and thus calls us to be separated unto Him. He calls us to be the light, to be an example to others so they too can experience a born-again life and enter His kingdom.

CHAPTER 8

The Church

Psalm 32:8–9 reads: "I will instruct you and teach you in the way you should go; I will guide you with My eye. Do not be like the horse or like the mule, which have no understanding, which must be harnessed with bit and bridle, else they will not come near you."

God, Your Instructor

When you are mature and living a holy life, God will instruct you and guide you—not your pastor, not your leader, but God Himself. Yes, He might use a pastor or leader to communicate to you or advise you, but God is the one who takes you by the hand on your daily walk.

God sent Samuel and Nathan to act as David's counselors, using them to communicate with David and instruct him. David understood that and respected these men of God, but he never worshiped them. He gave them proper place in his life, knowing they were God's servants.

David and Solomon

Studying the life of David and his son Solomon, we see that David took his sandals off before the Lord. Though he did slip a bit, he recognized he had done wrong in the sight of God, so he repented, acknowledged his sin, and asked for forgiveness. David feared the Lord and was forgiven for his sins.

Solomon, on the other hand, failed to completely remove his sandals. He did his own thing and followed other gods in his later years. At his second meeting with God, God was very specific with him about what he needed to do, but he failed to follow God's path. He decided to put his dirty sandals back on and walked unrighteously, serving other gods. As a result, the kingdom was divided, as we read in 1 Kings 11:9–13:

> The LORD became angry with Solomon because his heart had turned away from the LORD, the God of Israel, who had appeared to him twice. Although he had forbidden Solomon to follow other gods, Solomon did not keep the LORD's command. So the LORD said to Solomon, "Since this is your attitude and you have not kept my covenant and my decrees, which I commanded you, I will most certainly tear the kingdom away from you and give it to one of your subordinates. Nevertheless, for the sake of David your father, I will not do it during your lifetime. I will tear it out of the hand of your son. Yet I will not tear the whole kingdom from him, but will give him one tribe for the sake of David my servant and for the sake of Jerusalem, which I have chosen."

The saddest thing about Solomon's disobedience is that in spite of God's rebuke, there is no evidence that he repented, as did his father, David. Makes you wonder what his final destination was, doesn't it?

What a great lesson we can learn from this father-and-son duo. When we walk holy with the Lord, God's divine protection is with us all the time, but as soon as we deviate from God's way, we are on our own. How can the Spirit of God reside in an unrighteous, unclean temple? Though we believers are righteous in Christ Jesus, not all of us walk righteously in His presence. Our minds meditate on all sorts of things, but the minute we begin contemplating a certain temptation, we are setting ourselves up to sin. If we are not careful and strong in the Lord, we will fail and give in to that temptation.

Temptation is like the wind; it is always around us, always lurking to engulf us in its grasp. That's why Jesus told His disciples to pray so that they would not give in to temptation. The Bible further tells us to resist the devil and his temptations, and he will leave. You might ask how we can battle temptation. The only way to overcome temptation is by utilizing the sword of the Spirit, which is the Word of God, renewing our minds with it daily. Our bodies are weak; however, His Spirit is sufficient in us. He makes us strong in our weakness when we rely on Him. We therefore need to be connected to Him at all times. If we are not, we will truly fall into the trap of temptation.

The Upper Room

When Jesus ascended to heaven, He did not leave His disciples with a preacher, a pastor, or some other leader or person to guide them. No, He did none of that. He gave them the promise of the Holy Spirit, who was to come to them shortly and be their source of guidance and authority. He said He would not leave them orphans but would send the Holy Spirit, who would guide and teach them. This is an awesome promise from the Lord Himself. Read His words:

> If you love me, obey my commandments. And I will ask the Father, and he will give you another Advocate, who will never leave you. He is the Holy Spirit, who leads into all truth. The world cannot receive him, because it isn't looking for Him and doesn't recognize Him. But you know Him, because He lives with you now and later will be in you. No, I will not abandon you as orphans—I will come to you. Soon the world will no longer see me, but you will see me. Since I live, you also will live. When I am raised to life again, you will know that I am in my Father, and you are in me, and I am in you. Those who accept my commandments and obey them are the ones who love me. And because they love me, my Father will love them. And I will love them and reveal myself to each of them.
>
> John 14:15–21 NLT

In the book of Acts, we learn that this promise was fulfilled on the day of Pentecost when the Holy Spirit made His presence known to the disciples in the upper room. The Holy Spirit came in a new and powerful way that day. He is still here today, and He is here to stay. Throughout the Old Testament, we see that God the Holy Spirit made few appearances. But now that the promise has arrived, He is fully with us today. Receive Him, embrace Him, obey Him.

King David declared, "The Lord is my shepherd" (Psalm 23:1). The Lord alone is our shepherd. David saw that and understood it. Again, David did not call Samuel his pastor or shepherd. He admired and respected this son and servant of God, but he did not worship or idolize him. So must we be careful to do also.

My Pastor

About three years ago, I was talking to a friend, and he was bragging about the pastor of his church. He kept saying, "My pastor" this, and "My pastor" that. He sounded like he was idolizing him, and every time I heard him, I thought to myself, *Wow! I thought his pastor was God.* One year later, I saw him again, and he mentioned he was attending a new church and that he had a new pastor. He started telling the same story: "My pastor" this, and "My pastor" that. One year later, he was looking for a new pastor again. Maybe he was looking for a man to be his shepherd instead of looking to the true Shepherd.

Whom are you following? Whom are you worshiping and idolizing? Men are men, and they will always disappoint you. They will always let you down; they will do and say the wrong things. David understood this. He did not idolize Samuel but saw God at work through him. He gave him his proper place but never exalted him above God. Paul too understood this principle and taught the people at Corinth that their "faith should not be in the wisdom of men but in the power of God" (1 Corinthians 2:5).

Samuel was just a vessel used by God to communicate to God's servants, to His chosen ones. Samuel never attempted to take the place of God and never intended to be God either. He was merely God's servant and lived as such. Samuel understood that the ground where he walked was God's, not his. That is why he never pretended to be God or tried to take the place of God.

Physically, when we take our sandals off and walk on the ground, we become fully aware of how tender our feet are. When we are in that position, we pay close attention to where we place our feet. We carefully look ahead, fixing our sight on where to take our next step.

The same should be true in the spiritual realm. When we are walking on the ground God has entrusted us with—be it preaching, teaching, praise and worship, or something else—we need to be aware of how we do things. We must keep in mind that He is always there with us, around us, and in us.

The Church

The church is the last hope of the world. It is the last resource for someone who is looking for truth and answers to life. That is why God calls us to be separated unto Him, to walk with Him, to be consecrated to Him: so we can share His truth with others. This is what He means by walking on holy ground.

Sadly, many churches today are divided, practicing partiality and exhibiting jealousy, malice, and other wrong attitudes among their members and leaders. There is also much misuse of spiritual gifts. People need to learn how to use and polish the gift of ministry God has given them. The church must teach them how to use those gifts so that others can learn and grow and so that God our Father alone will be glorified.

Unfortunately, there is so much disunity, jealousy, and gossip within the church that the enemy is winning the battle and dividing us, causing many to jump from church to church. In the case with my friend who had a new pastor every year, I later found out that the churches he was attending demonstrated many of the problems already mentioned. It is sad because people are looking to belong, desiring to use their talents and gifts to glorify God. They want to go to church to listen and learn about the Bible and God, but when they see all we Christians do, they want nothing to do with church. Some remark, "Why should I go to your church, when I live a better life that most churchgoers?" Fair question, I think, that we Christians should answer.

The church represents the body of Christ. Therefore, I see myself as an ambassador of Christ and the church, and so are you. As Paul stated, "Now you are the body of Christ, and members individually" (1 Corinthians 12:27). In church nowadays, however, we see many "selfies," people who think that what they have is theirs. But as I usually tell people, the gospel is not for us to keep for ourselves, but rather for us to give away.

One of the problems I see in the church today is the large number of immature and uneducated leaders who don't know how to lead and communicate with others and think that the position they have within the church is theirs. When they see someone with talent and leadership abilities, they feel uncomfortable and threatened, fearing that their position will be given to another. A leader needs to grow and mature before being given responsibilities. Moses, for example, had some growing to do—in fact, forty years. Similarly, Joseph had to mature in obscurity more than ten years before he was given authority to deliver his people.

Identity

When we go to church today, instead of being filled with the Holy Spirit, we are filled with coffee! I attended a megachurch the other day, and in the lobby there was a Starbuck's coffee outlet. Coffee was being served before the service, during the service, and after the service. People were drinking coffee during praise and worship as well as during the preaching. All they needed was popcorn. The sanctuary had a big screen for showing videos, and they showed a clip that featured the *Late Show* and its new host. After the video clip, the preacher said, "I haven't missed a show and don't think I ever will!"

As ridiculous as this story sounds, it is very true. More and more, authenticity in churches is taking on the form of imitation. Identity is a major issue because the goal is not to reach the lost, but to entertain the community that the church lives in. I see churches all over the United States following the same idea to increase the number of attendees by entertaining rather than teaching and instructing toward righteous living. Such churches preach what the ear wants to hear rather than preach the truth. The emphasis is on preaching the love of God, but not what He hates—sin.

I was talking with a middle-aged woman the other day, and she mentioned that when she was a teenager, she was hungry to know more about God. Sadly, they were not teaching what she needed to know at the youth service she attended. One day she asked the youth pastor why they didn't teach the Bible instead of just having games and entertaining the kids. The youth pastor's response, she said, was, "If we do that, nobody will come." That was forty years ago—have you looked at church lately?

Joy is in the Word of God. Joy is in the Lord. Feed them God and they will be fed.

Our Identification

We were formed by God, deformed by sin, and transformed by the Spirit. We were given newness of life through the Son. Therefore, our identification is not found in the name of the church we attend or the denomination we belong to. Our identification on earth and heaven is found in Christ, and it has been sealed by the Holy Spirit in us (Ephesians 1:13).

Our identification on earth and heaven is Jesus Christ alone—not a church name or denomination. After the fall of man, our heavenly Father decided to redeem us, cleanse us, purify us, give us new life, and give us a chance to be born again. By the shedding of His blood, we were redeemed, cleansed, and forgiven. Only by the blood of Christ can we be His.

We are one in Christ; we have unity in Him. We also have peace, fellowship, abundance of blessings, joy, healing, provision, and all we could dream of. Through Christ alone, we receive the fullness of God, the Father for life.

To Jesus was given all authority in heaven and on earth. The authority given to the first Adam, Jesus now possesses. That authority is in place forever and ever. He holds it for eternity. It is the authority that only a holy and righteous God can keep and hold. Only in God through Jesus can we enter His kingdom and enjoy His promises and the blessings already prepared for those who love Him.

Again, your identification on earth and in heaven is Christ, not your church name or denomination. You are not going to go to Sao Paulo, Brazil, and identify yourself to Christians there as being from a specific church; this kind of identification has meaning only within that church. Rather, your identification is Jesus, who paid a ransom for you. As it is written, "But you were washed, but you were sanctified, but you were justified in the name of the Lord Jesus and by the Spirit of our God" (1 Corinthians 6:11).

CHAPTER 9

On Fire

At thirty-four years of age, he found himself serving the most high God, a young and energetic minister of the body of Christ. I was privileged to come to know him through a mutual friend. His physical appearance was not as handsome as he might have wished, but his spirit was all anyone could ever want—shining and peaceful, bold and sincere. The thing that caught my attention the first time I met him was that he said he was working on obtaining a location to hold church services. One year later, he had found a place in a strip mall, and I offered to help with the inside construction of partition walls, stage, storage space, and some other needed things.

Not Enough Help

One day I was working on the building when a middle-aged man approached me in the parking lot and asked, "What are you guys building? A store?"

"No," I replied, "we are building a church."

"Ahh," he exclaimed thoughtfully, and we began an interesting conversation. The man said, "I'm Catholic, and I own a botanic store in this strip mall. I don't understand why so many Christians, after they come out of a church service, come to my botanic and buy candles and other stuff from me. Is it that they have no faith?"

I tried to explain. "Well, Jesus said of some people, 'They honor me with their lips.'" I added, "Many have not yet developed a strong faith system that enables them to fully depend on God. They don't believe in the power of the Word of God, so they try to find other means to reinforce their belief."

Then he said, "You know, I don't get it. There are three churches in this strip mall alone and many more within a five-mile radius from here. It looks like it must be a good business for there to be so many of them. It sure looks like it's a good business, isn't it? Besides," he said, "churches demand people to give them 10 percent of their earnings. That's a good business to be in, right?"

I responded, "Do you know about tithes and offerings, that it is a commandment from God? God does not need our money. Everything is His, but He needs us to give, to help or invest in His kingdom. He want us to be part of it. He wants to bless us through our giving.

"Giving is like the law of gravity. It was established to do its work, and it applies to everyone. Tithing works the same. It is established to do its work. The measure we use to give is the same measure by which we will receive. Many don't have because they don't give. They are not generous with the increases God gives but want to keep it all for themselves. As a result, they end up in want, in debt, and in need."

Then the man said, "You know, lots of churches meet in what used to be a store. Why don't pastors and preachers look for a building instead of opening a storefront church?"

I answered, "Well, one of the reasons is that most people don't understand and don't want to give their tithes and offerings. If they did, there would be no need for many pastors to rent a storefront building to use as their church."

Just think about it. If people would give to God what is His, there would be lots of beautiful churches everywhere. However, many of us just want to keep everything God gives us to ourselves and retain His 10 percent for our own use, not realizing that when we give Him 10 percent of our earnings, we are still left with 90 percent. That percentage is now blessed and will likely last longer than 100 percent that is unblessed. When we don't give to God, we are robbing Him, as Malachi 3:8–9 warns. Do you want to rob God?

The person ended the conversation by saying, "You know what? You are different. I see that you love God. You have God in your heart, but many people out there just have God in their mouth. They say one thing but do the opposite. They preach one thing, but their actions are far from what they preach."

Quoting God's Word Only

The problem in today's society is just as it was in the Garden of Eden: we only quote God's Word, but we do not apply it. Look at the story in Genesis 3:1–3:

> The devil asked her, "Has God indeed said, 'You shall not eat of every tree of the garden'?"

> And the woman said to the serpent, "We may eat the fruit of the trees of the garden; but of the fruit of the tree which is in the midst of the garden, God has said, 'You shall not eat it, nor shall you touch it, lest you die.'"

Adam and Eve ended up doing what God had commanded them not to do. They chose to believe the lie spoken by the father of lies. They professed God's word but did not obey it.

Jesus too was questioned and tempted by the devil: "If you are the son of God . . ." (Matthew 4:3), thus challenging His identity and authority. In your walk with God, you will be questioned. Your authority will also be questioned. You will be confronted by evil opposition. Jesus did not respond by saying, "Yes, I am the Son of God." He responded with the Word of God; He responded by telling the devil that man is not sustained by bread alone, but by every word that comes forth from the mouth of God.

In the Garden of Eden, however, the decision Eve made reaped grievous consequences: her firstborn son killed his brother. In the garden after the fall, Adam and Eve might have asked, "God, why did You allow that to happen?" or "Why us, God?" Was their fall an act of God? Was that disastrous incident from God, or was it an act of the devil, who gained headway into their lives and into the young world in order to destroy it and keep it for himself?

Many times, when faced with opposition, our first response towards God is to ask, "Why me, God?" Many times we get upset with Him, as though He were punishing us. But no, everything that happens to us is a result of our decisions and actions.

God told Adam and Eve not to eat of the tree, but they did it anyway. They willfully disobeyed the mandate of the Lord God. We, too, often know what to do or not to do, but we disobey anyway and as a result must face the consequences, pain, sickness, lack, and so on. The results of disobedience are not from God. Jesus came to set us free from all that. He is our ticket to freedom from deception, sickness, sin—you name it. Receive Him, follow Him, remain in Him, and serve Him in holiness and in truth.

On Fire

The church needs to be on fire. But the only way the church can be on fire is if someone on fire fires it up. The church needs someone with the Spirit of the Lord in him. Joseph was filled with the Spirit of God and changed a nation. Paul, too, was filled with the Spirit and revolutionized Christianity. He spread the teachings of the Lord, thus demonstrating his faith.

To recognize faith, you must first understand it. What is faith? "Now faith is the substance of things hoped for, the evidence of things not seen. . . . By faith we understand that the worlds were framed by the word of God, so that the things which are seen were not made of things which are visible" (Hebrews 11:1, 3).

You might wonder what it is you need to have faith in. Well, you must have faith in God first and then faith in people. Pharaoh understood and ultimately had faith in Joseph's God. He saw in Joseph the hand of God at work because everything he put his hands on flourished. When there is no faith, there is no change.

Oh, why do you marvel at the work of God in a person, the way He uses the simple to show His great power? Who was Isaiah?

Who was Jeremiah? Who was Peter? Who was Matthew, Paul, Mary, King David, or Joseph? Jesus Himself was a carpenter, and I am a contractor. What are you? God can use you right where you are. Scripture reminds us, "For this very purpose I have raised you up, that I may show My power in you, and that My name may be declared in all the earth" (Romans 9:17).

The eyes of the flesh do not think twice to judge, but the eyes of the Spirit see an opportunity for a soul winner. The heart of the fool is quick to envy, but the pure in heart rejoice at the power of God in others to accomplish His will. They rejoice and thank God when they see the accomplishments of others.

Teaching Versus Preaching

First Corinthians 2:5 says, "Your faith should not be in the wisdom of men but in the power of God." However, there is a lot of confusion in the world today. There is so much preaching, so much talk. People's ears are saturated with lots of talk and lots of ideas from many outside sources, but there's not much revelation in the talk.

Many people direct their lives based on the knowledge and opinions of man rather than on the revelation of God. Jesus was called Teacher because He taught the word of the Father, which is the Word of God. He did not just talk it, but He walked it. Today there are many talkers, but few walkers.

When a preacher starts his message by saying, "Millions and millions of years ago . . ." run! Who knows what heathen book he might be reading to make such a statement? Millions and millions of years—is he for real? Only an atheist would make such a statement. If we are going to base our faith solely on the Bible, then let's start there. The problem today is too much preaching and not enough teaching.

Although the apostle Paul did not personally walk with Jesus like the other disciples did, the Lord transformed him and overshadowed him with His Spirit when he encountered Jesus on the road to Damascus. After that amazing change of heart, Paul not only preached but also taught the Word of God—he taught Jesus! Paul walked the talk. Paul was a teacher, not just a preacher. Anyone can talk or preach, but that doesn't mean they have had a transformation of heart or revelation of the Word (Jesus). That comes only from God the Father.

Paul developed other leaders, such as Timothy, Philemon, and others. He did not just develop followers, but he commissioned developing leaders to lead. Today, however, many people are into creating and having followers, even though the Great Commission says to go into all nations and make disciples.

If you compare Paul with Peter, you will see that Peter did not duplicate himself, like Paul did. Jesus duplicated Himself and trained twelve men right from the start, and we should do likewise. Character is what separates leadership; a true leader leads effectively from the Word of God. "He will stand tall in his shepherd-rule by God's strength, centered in the majesty of God-Revealed" (Micah 5:4 MSG).

A few months ago, I met a lady in her early sixties. She had come for help because she was going through some tough times. When I talked with her, I asked about her faith. To my surprise, she responded, "My faith is so shaky right now. Sometimes I feel I do not have any faith."

I felt sorry for her; then I said, "May I ask what happened?"

She said, "I have a brother who is a cardinal, and his messages and speeches are so convincing, so eloquent. He speaks with the right tone of voice and is so explicit. But when he comes out of the pulpit and is out of church, he is a different person. His actions, his way of living, and his way of treating others are shameful. Because of him, I do not believe in God and have no faith." She added, "My husband feels the same way. In fact, he doesn't go to church and doesn't even want to know about church and God anymore." By this time, tears were streaming from her eyes.

After listening carefully to what she had to say, I asked, "Can I share something with you? I feel that your eyes and faith have been put on men—not God."

I then explained to her that men will fall—always. No matter their denomination, many church leaders today are repeating the same mistakes over and over again. Why? It is simply because they do not know God. They preach God but don't know Him. They have no revelation. All they preach is in the natural; they are good talkers. What they need is a reencounter with Jesus, just like His disciples experienced. In order to understand Him and be able to listen to His voice, they need to meet the resurrected Christ again.

Just remember, it is He who chooses us and calls us, just like He called by name His twelve disciples. A true follower of truth is known by two things and two things alone, which the Lord Himself told us: (1) Love the Lord your God with all your heart, and (2) love others as you love yourself. That's it! That's all we need to do. Out of these two new commandments from our High Priest flow all the Law and the Prophets.

CHAPTER 10

His Word

If you think that the Old Testament is only a thing of the past, think again! The One who was from the beginning came quoting the Old Testament Scripture, and not only quoting it, but also walking in it and fulfilling it. As He said, "It is written, 'Man shall not live by bread alone, but by every word that proceeds from the mouth of God'" (Matthew 4:4). Notice He said "every word"—not just a few, and certainly not just the ones we think apply to us or the ones we feel more inclined to follow.

"All Scripture is inspired by God and is useful to teach us what is true and to make us realize what is wrong in our lives. It corrects us when we are wrong and teaches us to do what is right. God uses it to prepare and equip his people to do every good work" (2 Timothy 3:16–17 NLT). The Message translation of the same scripture puts it this way: "There's nothing like the written Word of God for showing you the way to salvation through faith in Christ Jesus. Every part of Scripture is God-breathed and useful one way or another—showing us truth, exposing our rebellion, correcting our mistakes, training us to live God's way. Through the Word we are put together and shaped up for the tasks God has for us."

As leaders and followers of the Lord God, we should know the power, majesty, and sovereignty of God Almighty in His Word. We know His love for us, that He is for us and wants the best for us. He has given all things to us so that we can live our lives in peace, harmony, abundance, and holiness. It is our choice to follow His lead or to ignore it. God has given us His Word, His love, and ultimately His Son to teach us His Word and the way we ought to live our lives for His glory. We are to bring Him glory in every step we take.

If we look closely at our role model, our high priest Jesus Christ, we see that He came as humbly as He could, with no riches or material possessions. He came in love and full of power and authority from God the Father. He came using the Word of God to empower, to heal, to feed, to rebuke, to exhort, to teach, and to proclaim the kingdom of God.

John 1:17 says, "For the law was given through Moses; grace and truth came through Jesus Christ." Moses heard the words of God in person, and God gave Him the ability to put them into writing. God also gave Moses the two stone tablets with the Ten Commandments. Why would God use people to write the Bible, our instruction book? Well, just like we use pens and pencils to write down important information, God used man to record His words. If you think about it, which has more power when we write something: we or the pen? Looking at it from that perspective, who has more power in the writing of the Bible: God or man?

The Word of God, the Bible, is like a puzzle. The more time you spend in it, the clearer the picture becomes. You will find that in the Old Testament, Jesus is sometimes referred to as the Angel of the Lord, and in the New Testament, He is the Spirit of the Lord. The Spirit of the Lord dwells in all those who love Him.

How is your love for Him? After all, He said, "Love God with all your heart, mind, and soul."

His Words

The words of God are so powerful, but until we understand the magnitude of their power—how magnificent, accurate, and powerful they are—we will not comprehend them. God is a God of greatness, power, and sovereignty. Everything He says will come to pass.

Have you noticed that God has already established all things? When I say *all things*, I literally mean "all things." Since the beginning of time, He created the heavens, the firmament, the earth, the moon, the sun—all things visible and invisible. He created them by speaking them into existence. For example, when He said, "Let there be light," there was light, and so on. "By the word of the Lord the heavens were made, and by the breath of His mouth all their host. He gathers the waters of the sea together as a heap; He lays up the deeps in storehouses. Let all the earth fear the Lord; let all the inhabitants of the world stand in awe of Him. For He spoke, and it was done; He commanded, and it stood fast" (Psalm 33:6–9). All living things hold on to God and are subject to Him, so why not man?

When Adam and Eve disobeyed God, His words did not prove void. When He confronted them, I believe He was a disappointed because of what they had done in the garden and suddenly became angry, just like we parents do when our children disobey us. Remember what God asked them: "What is this you have done?" I believe God was disgusted and upset because of their disobedience, and thus curses were spoken to the pair. He spoke into existence all creation as well as man's curses because of his disobedience. That tells us that all His words are alive. God said in Deuteronomy 30:19, "I have set before you life and death, blessing and cursing; therefore choose life."

The Holy Bible, in Ephesians 4:26, also reminds us, "'In your anger do not sin': Do not let the sun go down while you are still angry" (NIV).

Guarding Our Words

We need to learn to guard the words we speak to our children because in the same way that God spoke and brought the world into existence, the words that come out of our mouths will not return void. They will take root, and if they were not good words, they will come back hounding us with what we have already said. For example, if a father tells his son, "You are good for nothing," or "You are so dumb," the little boy grows up feeling and acting exactly as his father described him. Similarly, God's words are recorded in our hearts and minds. As soon as we speak them, they are sent to accomplish His purpose.

I know of a man who is now a mature adult. When he was a child, he grew up with his aunts and cousins, mainly girls. Because he was around girls all the time, he was told he acted like one. He was called "girly" and told, "You sit just like a girl. You talk like a girl, you cry like a girl, and you walk like a girl." Guess what? Unsurprisingly, this boy grew up developing the mind of a girl, and as a result, he was confused about his sexual identity. From the words spoken to him, he developed a girly attitude and female ways.

Life and death are indeed in the power of the tongue.

After Isaac blessed Jacob instead of Esau, Esau asked his father to bless him too. Isaac refused, saying that the blessing had already been spoken. Then Esau begged him for any blessing at all. But the words had already been spoken, and Jacob received the blessing that should have been Esau's.

There are many promises in the Holy Bible and lots of mysteries in the Word of God. Remember, the Word became flesh, and the Word is alive, the Word is Jesus Christ. One of the reasons we do not exercise or experience the promises Jesus gave us is that our faith is smaller than a mustard seed. Jesus asks us to have only a little faith—small faith. In fact, He said, "I tell you the truth, if you had faith even as small as a mustard seed, you could say to this mountain, 'Move from here to there,' and it would move. Nothing would be impossible" (Matthew17:20 NLT). In addition, Jesus told us that greater things we would do than what He did (see John 14:12). Is that a statement or a commandment? That is a promise, and it comes with authority.

We have been given the same authority Jesus had when He was resurrected. We can speak God's Word into our lives. Again, let's remember what He said in Matthew 4:4: "Man shall not live by bread alone, but by every word that proceeds from the mouth of God." We can speak things into existence, things like healing for ourselves and others, provision, protection, and so on. I'm not talking about pursuing financial gain, calling in riches. No, I'm saying we should call in the promises God has already given us, claiming and receiving His will for our lives, similar to the way Jesus commanded the storm to cease and it obeyed Him.

For example, one day I was at home with my daughter, who was only seven years old at the time. A storm hit our area that day, with lots of wind, rain, and thunder. We could look out the window and see the tall pine trees swinging from side to side. They looked as if they were about to snap and fall onto the house.

I told my daughter, "Let's pray and cast the storm out!" She was used to praying with my wife and me, so we started praying. Our eyes were closed, but in the midst of praying, I stole a glimpse at her, seeing her little body and hand moving and rebuking that storm, telling it to go away. I felt her big faith, and minutes later that ferocious storm abated. It ceased completely, praise the Lord! Not only are the words we speak powerful, but also the faith and conviction that the Word of God is true. Faith in God's promise unleashed the movement in the midst of the storm. Faith in God's Word makes things happen.

Another time my family and I were traveling to Orlando, Florida. It was raining, and as we entered the city limits of Buena Vista, the rain intensified and the road visibility diminished. I started to pray and cast out the rain, and believe it or not, the rain rapidly disappeared. My belief in God and the faith system I had developed caused the rain dissipate, just like Jesus said would happen when He said, "If you tell this mountain move and be cast into the sea, it will obey you." Amen!

I received confirmation of God's act on our behalf when I called my aunt in Orlando. She said, "Rob, it looks like you've brought the sun with you. It has been raining for the past few days, and rain was expected for the rest of the week, but it just stopped raining."

I exclaimed, "Wow!" and looking to heaven I said, "Thank You, Lord."

Do you have any mountains or storms obstructing your life that need to be removed? Remove them! Jesus has given you power and authority over them.

I like the movie *The Incredibles*. There are quite a few scenes to learn from, but one I especially like concerns a little girl who has the power to disappear and to build a shield of protection. In this scene, her mom had told her not to use the superpowers she possessed because they were among civilians, but when they get into trouble and her mom commands her to use all her power, she does not know how and is afraid to even try. That is how we are. We have been given power and authority but don't know how to use it and are afraid to even try. As a result, we seldom use it, and even when we do make an attempt, we use it in unbelief and nothing happens.

His Work Is His Story

Psalm 33:6, 9 says, "By the word of the LORD the heavens were made, and all the host of them by the breath of His mouth. . . . For He spoke, and it was done; He commanded, and it stood fast." What a workmanship it was! He did all things perfectly— the entire creation was perfect. What a magnificent day it was when He created man. He created us to reproduce and to till and work the land. Six days He worked to establish everything for the present, the future, and all generations to come.

The Bible tells us that a thousand years on earth is as one day in heaven (Psalm 90:4). Therefore, it has been only two days in God's sight since Jesus, His only begotten Son, was with us. That also means it has been only a few days, not millions and millions of years, since the creation of the earth.

Oh God, who could be more powerful than You? There is none like You! You are the creator of everything. Who am I to question You? Who am I to run away from You, oh Lord? Who am I to disobey You? You are everywhere, and You see all things. You are like the air around us, which we can't see, but we can feel. That air exists everywhere and travels from sea to sea, from coast to coast, from north to south, from east to west. You are the one who lights up our path, cleanses us, and purifies our thoughts, our minds, our hearts, and our bodies. Let it be You, Lord, who directs our thinking and directs our walk. Let it be You, oh Lord, whom we live for. You call us sons and daughters; keep us that way. You are the one who clothes us, protects us, and provides for us. You are the one who keeps us standing and gives us new strength each day. You are the one who sustains us and keeps us breathing Your breath of life.

To know You, Lord, is a privilege. To know You is humbling. To know You is a pleasure. To know You is life. To know You is to love You. To know You is everything to me, and My joy and trust are in You.

Now that I have found You, Lord, I want to walk with You forever. You are so loving. You are my comforter, my light, my guide, my life, my protection. You are my Lord, whom I was missing all my life.

I understand now that life without You is in vain. My life without You is nothing. I have no power, no control of things. I have learned that it is You who gives me strength and empowers me to do all things.

Heavenly Father, Thank You for permitting me to be in Your presence. Thank You for letting Yourself be known to me. I thank You for Your Son, whom You sent to destroy the works of the enemy, who came and took all things back for You. All authority You have given Him. I thank You for Your Holy Spirit, that promise You gave us when you said, "I will not leave you orphans; I will come to you" (John 14:18). He is the helper who will walk with us always. It is through your Holy Spirit that we can feel You; we cannot see You, but we can feel You.

You are my Father, and I know that I'm not Your only child. There are many like me who have chosen to walk with You and talk to You and hear Your voice. You are our Father, and I thank You for being there for us. We love You and adore You.

Father, I love Your Word. Before I look at it, I know the beginning and the end, because You are the beginning and the end. I love the endless mysteries found in Your Word, but I'm more blessed with the revelations of your great name that I receive day by day. When I read Your Word, it fills me, and I just feel like running to You. It makes me feel so close to You that I can sense You breathing on me. You are the great I AM, and in You are life and eternal living. You are the Way, You are the Truth, and You are the Life. I love You with all my heart.

What Is in Your Heart?

Out of the abundance of the heart, the mouth speaks. We repeat whatever we learn from the things we hear, see, read, and experience, not realizing that whatever we say can bring death or life. Once again, Matthew 4:4 reminds us, "It takes more than bread to stay alive. It takes a steady stream of words from God's mouth" (MSG).

With that being said, what are we speaking? Is it defeat, deceit, gossip, deception, lack, or some other such thing ? We choose the television programs and movies we will watch and the music we will listen to. Did you know that all of these things influence our minds and hearts, that ultimately everything we learn from them comes out of our mouths? Yes, it is voluntary— we choose. We do and say things unconsciously because we have not yet come to life; we are still dead in trespasses, transgressions, and sin, separated from our Lord.

Again, in Matthew 4:4, Jesus was quoting from and fulfilling the word of God from the book of Deuteronomy, chapter 8, verses 2–3: "And you shall remember that the LORD your God led you all the way these forty years in the wilderness, to humble you and test you, to know what was in your heart, whether you would keep His commandments or not. So He humbled you, allowed you to hunger, and fed you with manna which you did not know nor did your fathers know, that He might make you know that man shall not live by bread alone; but man lives by every word that proceeds from the mouth of the LORD." Later in His ministry, Jesus indeed lived on every word that came out of the mouth of God. Jesus used God's word to heal, deliver, resurrect, and empower others.

The message is this: whenever you want to say something, think before you say it. Choose words that edify, words that encourage, words that uplift, words that speak truth. Humankind has been given a choice from the beginning of time. In the garden, Adam and Eve chose death instead of life. Because of that one decision, all generations were affected. The decision you make today, good or bad, will affect both you and future generations. Choose your words wisely—choose life!

Prayer of Faith

"The word is near you, in your mouth and in your heart" (that is, the word of faith which we preach)" (Romans 10:8). Prayer is simply talking with God; it's sharing with Him whatever is on your heart. It's sharing with Him how you feel and the way you feel about your family, friends and others. It's communicating with Him all the things you see that are wrong and how you would like them to be different. It's asking Him how He feels about you and what His plans and purpose are for your life.

When you pray to God, you are focused on who He is and who you are in relation to Him. When you talk to God, He begins to show you more and more who He made you to be and what He wants you to do. Just remember that when you talk to God, the communication has two parts: (1) talking and (2) listening. Don't be just a talker, but also listen to the voice of God and obey it. So many times we are so focused on talking that we miss out on what God wants to say to us.

When you pray, you develop openness with the Lord. The more you pray, the more comfortable you feel with Him and the closer you feel to Him as well. When you start to be open and transparent with Him, you live more boldly and securely.

77

If you would like to receive Jesus into your life or recommit your life to Him, just say these words:

God, I'm here today acknowledging that I'm a sinner. I have disobeyed You in so many ways. I believe that You sent Your Son, Jesus Christ, to save me and set me free from my wrongdoing. Jesus, I ask You to forgive me of all my sins. I ask You to redeem me and cleanse me. I receive You as my Lord and Savior. I need You to purify me inside and out, dwell in me, empower me, and direct my path—mind, body, and soul. I ask You to be my Lord and Savior today and forever. In Jesus' name I pray. Amen.

Romans 10:8, which says, "The word is near you, in your mouth and in your heart" (that is, the word of faith which we preach)," is a mystery that is hard for human flesh to understand. To the spirit man, however, it is so clear, and it's all we need in order to be saved. God's words are so powerful. He created all things by speaking them into being, and everything came to life. He used those words in the same way we use ours, because His words are life.

When we accept Jesus into our lives, we need to start speaking life, as He gives us that life, that abundant life. When you start speaking His words and walking with Him, you might seem weird and somehow out of this world to your family and friends. Don't let that stop you! Yes, you are different—not better than others, but different. The evil things of this world will not interest you anymore, things such as bad programs on TV, pornography, lying, or listening to bad music. It is normal to feel uncomfortable and out of place, because you are now in a different realm, the spirit realm. Your eyes have been opened to see the light, and you have been given the Holy Spirit, who leads you into that light and keeps you there. You can now see things from God's perspective.

Others have not yet received what you already have: a close relationship with Jesus. As a result, others cannot understand what you do. They are still living in darkness. Your job is to shine your light into their darkness by living a life of example, glorifying God in every step you take and in all that you do.

Your new job has started. You are now an ambassador for Christ. You have been called from darkness into light. You have been given a new life. It is your job to spread that light and guide others to have newness of life as well.

You may not feel comfortable by this new change, but remember this: The Lord God is always with you. He is the one who, if you have something to say, will give you the words to speak. Many times the words He gives you are words that come out of the Bible; this is His Spirit talking to you and through you. He records His words in your heart. That is why it is so important to read His Word and meditate on it day and night, so that when we need it, it is there.

Will you miss out on life because you no longer do what others who do not know the truth do? Absolutely not! In fact, you will enjoy life even more. Besides a new life, you now have joy, peace, and the blessed assurance that can be obtained only by coming to Jesus Christ. Your life has meaning and purpose; God gives you direction and leads you into everything you need to do. You will also discover other abilities that you did not know you possessed.

God's promise to us is, "Eye has not seen, nor ear heard . . . the things which God has prepared for those who love Him" (1 Corinthians 2:9). Everything is established. All things have been made, and all we need to do is receive those promises and apply them to our lives.

CHAPTER 11

Give Up to Go Up

It is one thing to listen to God's voice, but it is another to obey Him. Many of us profess the Word of the Lord, but sadly, not all of us do what we preach. When we do, however, we are powerful. If our shoes are completely off our feet and we are walking a holy life, we are empowered by the majesty of God Almighty.

Unfortunately, this kind of holiness is missing, not only in the world today, but also in the church. Obedience plays a large role in this. "Obedience to what?" you may ask. Obedience to God, doing what He calls us to do. We live in an *I* world and thus miss out on serving others, including God. We are so focused on ourselves that although we might hear the voice of God, we don't always do what He says. Luke 6:46 warns us about this: "But why do you call Me 'Lord, Lord,' and not do the things which I say?"

True men of God are missing in the world today. I'm not talking about men of position, but real men of God who love Him, listen to His words, and obey Him. There are many stories in the Bible about true men of God. Let me share a couple.

First is the prophet Elijah. When he was in a cave and God commanded him to go anoint Hazael as king over Syria and also to anoint Elisha as prophet, he immediately went to do it. He did not hesitate or think about it twice. Elijah just obeyed and executed the word of God, unlike Jonah, who was sent but did not obey. Jonah took a different route, an opposite route from what God had told him to take. He kept his sandals on, walking in his direction, not God's

We can see in this how the power of God is manifested in those who obey Him. A man of God who is empowered by God Himself can command fire to come down from heaven and fire will come down. He can also command rain to stop and have it obey him. A man of God will heal people and uplift, encourage, and lead them to their maker, their God. A man of God is noticed from afar, and he can do all thing through the Lord who empowers him.

Another good example is Elisha. Elisha was a man of humble beginnings; his profession, according to the Bible, was that of farmer: "Elisha . . . was plowing with twelve yoke of oxen before him" (1 Kings 19:19). Before God called him to greatness, he was just an ordinary person. But it is ordinary people like Elisha—and like you and me—who are empowered by God, who wait on His promises, who listen and do what God calls them to do.

If you heard God's voice speaking the following words to you, what would you do? This is what God told Elijah: "Go, return on your way to the Wilderness of Damascus; and when you arrive . . . Elisha the son of Shaphat of Abel Meholah you shall anoint as prophet in your place" (1 Kings 19:15–16). Anoint someone in your place? Would you do that, pastor? Would you do that, leader? Would you do that, man of God? Would you obey the voice of God if He commanded you to anoint someone in your place?

You probably would not. Think about it for a moment. To anoint someone in your place would probably be the end of you. That would probably be the last thing you would want to do. But forget about looking for someone to replace you. Just go and anoint someone, empower someone, help someone, uplift someone, encourage someone, would you? I tell you, we pray almost every day for more laborers, but when they come, we don't recognize them and offer no help. That is what we are missing in the world today: Leaders looking for new leaders so they can recognize, uplift, and anoint all those who are already appointed and empowered by God.

Just remember, when you give up your position, give it to another as instructed by God. God will elevate you for your obedience. Elijah was not full of himself. If he had been, he would have refused to do what God told him to do. However, by faith he obeyed, and God rewarded that obedience by giving him a much better position—in heaven. Elijah's position only got better.

For this act of obedience, Elijah had to deny himself. He gave up the world but was given the reward of eternal life in the mansion already prepared for him. Elijah was elevated to higher ground, to a higher platform. He was elevated to be on high, to be in the presence of our Father God.

What if Elijah had refused to obey God? Can you picture it? Just meditate on it for a minute. Elijah is in a cave in the desert, with no food or drink, God calls him, but he doesn't obey. He doesn't want to give up his position—he wants to keep it. He doesn't want to anoint someone else in his place as God commanded him. If he had chosen that path, I believe he would have starved to death because of his disobedience to the voice and command of God. God would probably have distanced Himself from Elijah, and Elijah would have missed the greater reward and position that God had for him. But that is not what happened. Elijah acted in faith, just like Abraham did when he was told to sacrifice his only beloved son, Isaac.

What is God telling you to do today? To give up your position? Your fame? Some of your money? Only if you are able to hear God's voice can you truly do what He asks of you. Only someone who knows and follows the Lord can do this.

Elijah gave up himself, the world, and his position, but in the end he won the crown of life. He never knew death because he was taken straight up to heaven. Later we see him in the transfiguration with Jesus and Moses. Do you think for one moment that Elijah missed out on the world? Did he miss out on life?

We can also see the transformation of his successor, Elisha, who immediately took his sandals off his feet to serve God and others. The empowerment Elisha received was double that of Elijah's. He was a man of God, not only because of what he stood for and what he said, but because of his obedience to do what God called him to do. A man of God will always do what God is asking him to do, whether it makes sense or not. He is moved by faith.

Giving Up to Go Up

In the same manner, Jesus gave up everything to come to earth and show us the way. As a result, He was mightily exalted by the Father. Living in human flesh, when it was time for Him to give up His life, He felt the heavy cup of bitterness, that filthy cup that contained all of man's sins and transgressions, bearing down on His shoulders. At that moment, He felt desolate and far from the Father.

Elijah, Elisha, Jesus, and other men of God had no material possessions, so you might think it would be easy for them to give up everything. That, however, is a short-sighted view. Elijah did not own a single thing. Jesus, speaking of Himself, said, "Foxes have holes and birds of the air have nests, but the Son of Man has nowhere to lay His head" (Matthew 8:20). He also said, "Do not lay up for yourselves treasures on earth, where moth and rust destroy and where thieves break in and steal; but lay up for yourselves treasures in heaven, where neither moth nor rust destroys and where thieves do not break in and steal. For where your treasure is, there your heart will be also" (Matthew 6:19–21).

When we leave this earth, we will not take any material thing with us. The only things we take are the intangible rewards accumulated over the course of our years. When we gave a helping hand, when we did what God called us to do, when someone else's life is better off because we lived—all these will reap an eternal reward. When we focus on others rather than just ourselves, we are taken care of. When our eyes are off ourselves and set on someone else, God will provide for us.

I knew a multimillionaire who passed away two years ago. I do not know where or with whom he left all his material possessions; I do not know the details of how he disposed of his estate. But one thing I know for sure: from all his possessions, he took nothing to heaven with him. I do know he went to heaven, because he was a devoted Christian who understood God and had developed a strong personal relationship with Christ. He was someone who, I believe, took his sandals off his feet and walked connected with the Lord at all times. He also did many things for the kingdom, impacted many lives, and touched the hearts of people and led them to the Lord. Those are the only things he took with him to heaven. He was a man of God who, when sharing the kingdom of God, talked with power and authority. He talked about the Lord as if He were near Him and as if He really knew Him—and he did. Now, I believe, he is in a special room that was prepared for him by God, the giver of life. His life could be summed up with this verse: "The fruit of the righteous is a tree of life, and he who wins souls is wise" (Proverbs 11:30).

Man of God

A man of God is not known by what he says, but by his likeness to the Son of God. He walks righteously, the light in him shining brightly on others around him. His walk is straight, humble, and empowered.

A man of God is filled with the Spirit of God and carries His sword. When he walks to the marketplace or anywhere else, people take notice that he is a true servant of God. "A tree is identified by its fruit. If a tree is good, its fruit will be good. If a tree is bad, its fruit will be bad" (Matthew 12:33 NLT).

A man of God speaks truth. Words of edification, affirmation, encouragement, wisdom, and power come out of his mouth. A true man of God is one who obediently seeks Him and does His will. Just listening and quoting Scriptures is not enough; we need to obey the Word and do what He calls us to do.

In the Old Testament, a person who was devoted to God was called a "man of God." In Hebrew, this was another word for "prophet." He was someone who had gained that title, not by what he said, but because he was an ambassador for God. He was a passionate ally with God, obeying His voice and serving Him at all times. The prophet Elisha is referred to in the Bible as a man of God.

According to the New Testament, there are now only sons and daughters of God. We are all God's creation, but not all have earned the sonship title. That is given by God the Father and obtained only through Jesus Christ. As it is written:

> But to all who did receive Him, who believed in his name, he gave the right to become children of God.
>
> John 1:12

> For you are all sons of God through faith in Christ Jesus.
>
> Galatians 3:26

> And since we are his children, we are his heirs. In fact, together with Christ we are heirs of God's glory. But if we are to share his glory, we must also share his suffering. Yet what we suffer now is nothing compared to the glory he will reveal to us later. For all creation is waiting eagerly for that future day when God will reveal who his children really are.
>
> Romans 8:17–19 NLT

The Spirit Himself bears witness with our spirit that we are children of God.

Romans 8:16

Jesus sealed this when He taught us to how to pray to our heavenly Father:

> But you, when you pray, go into your room, and when you have shut your door, pray to your Father who is in the secret place; and your Father who sees in secret will reward you openly. And when you pray, do not use vain repetitions as the heathen do. For they think that they will be heard for their many words.
>
> Therefore do not be like them. For your Father knows the things you have need of before you ask Him. In this manner, therefore, pray:

> Our Father in heaven,
> Hallowed be Your name.
> Your kingdom come.
> Your will be done
> On earth as it is in heaven.
> Give us this day our daily bread.
> And forgive us our debts,
> As we forgive our debtors.
> And do not lead us into temptation,
> But deliver us from the evil one.
> For Yours is the kingdom and the power and the glory forever. Amen.

For if you forgive men their trespasses, your heavenly Father will also forgive you. But if you do not forgive men their trespasses, neither will your Father forgive your trespasses.

Matthew 6:6–15

When we are newly born in Christ, we are created anew in spirit, separated for Him and representing Him as His children. How does a mom or dad feel when their children are obedient and develop great communication and friendship with them? They feel proud. But how about disobedient children, who are the opposite of good? How do their parents feel about them? It's the same way with God. He rejoices when He finds someone who obeys and walks in His ways, someone He can call his son or daughter.

CHAPTER 12

Out of This World

As God's children, we all must remember that He expects us to behave as such. He will direct us and correct us "because the Lord disciplines the one he loves, and he chastens everyone he accepts as his son" (Hebrew 12:6 NIV). God abhors sin. Don't get me wrong—He loves the sinner, but not the sin. He so loved the world that He gave His only begotten Son to rescue the sinner and bring him to a new life—a transformed life, a life out of this world's system, a life walking in holiness, a life moved out of darkness and into His marvelous light.

We are in the world but not of it. Those are the words of our Lord Jesus to us in John 17:14–15: "I have given them Your word; and the world has hated them because they are not of the world, just as I am not of the world. I do not pray that You should take them out of the world, but that You should keep them from the evil one." Jesus was praying for us, not to be taken from the world, but to be protected from the evil one who rules the world. But many so-called brethren are in the world and blend in with it—looking, acting, drinking, marrying, and living just like the rest of the world. When that happens, whom are they serving and living for? Well, their actions reveal what they are; their true identity is in their actions. From their actions, they can be recognized from afar.

In the World, But Out of It

"How can God's children be in the world, but not of the world?" you may ask. To answer that, let's look first at this scripture from 1 John 5:19: "We know that we are children of God and that the world around us is under the control of the evil one."

When we read of the "world" in the New Testament, we are reading the Greek word *cosmos. Cosmos* most often refers to the inhabited earth and the people who live in it apart from God. The Bible tells us that Satan is the ruler of this cosmos. By the simple realization that the word *world* refers to a world system ruled by Satan, we can more readily appreciate Jesus Christ's claims that God's children are no longer of the world. In other words, as born-again Christians, we are no longer ruled by sin, nor are we bound by the principles of the world. That is why it is written, "He who sins is of the devil, for the devil has sinned from the beginning. For this purpose the Son of God was manifested, that He might destroy the works of the devil. Whoever has been born of God does not sin, for His seed remains in him; and he cannot sin, because he has been born of God" (1 John 3:8–9). In addition, we are being transformed into the image of Christ daily, causing our interest in the things of the world to become less and less as we mature in Christ.

In other words, we are physically present in the world—but not of it. We are set apart for God; we are not part of this world's system and its values ruled by evil. We learn this from Christ Himself when He said to God the Father:

> Now I'm returning to you. I'm saying these things in the world's hearing so my people can experience my joy completed in them. I gave them your word; the godless world hated them because of it, because they didn't join the world's ways, just as I didn't join the world's ways.
>
> I'm not asking that you take them out of the world but that you guard them from the Evil One.
>
> They are no more defined by the world than I am defined by the world. Make them holy—consecrated—with the truth; your word is consecrating truth. In the same way that you gave me a mission in the world, I give them a mission in the world. I'm consecrating myself for their sakes so they'll be truth-consecrated in their mission.
>
> John 17:14–15 MSG

As dear children of God, we should be separated from the influence of this world's system. This is the direct command from God Himself to all His children: to be holy and live a holy, righteous life; to be set apart from the influence of evil and its followers—to completely take our sandals off our feet. We should not engage in the sinful activities the world promotes, things such as lying, hatred, jealousy, envy, fornication, adultery, and sorcery, nor are we to retain the characterless, corrupt mind that the world creates and promotes.

We need to abide in the Lord and be conformed by His Spirit, who guides and comforts us in our daily walk. We are to offer ourselves as living sacrifices and renew our minds daily to that of Jesus Christ. We need to understand that we live in a spiritual realm and are confronted on a day-to-day basis with things we do not see or understand. Such things can be grasped only by the Holy Spirit, who overshadows us, protects us, and reveals to us the things to come, giving us discernment and protection in the battles we cannot fight in our own flesh.

Lastly, being in the world but not of it is necessary if we are to be a light to those who are in spiritual darkness and bondage. We are to live in such a way that the rest of the world will see the reflection of the Lord Jesus Christ in us through our good deeds and behavior. They should notice that there is something different about us. Christians who live, think, and act like those who do not know Christ do Him a great disservice. Even the heathen know that a tree is known by its fruit. As Christians, we should exhibit the fruit of the Spirit within us at all times—full-time, not just partial or when it is to our favor or convenience.

The Lightbulb

One morning I received a revelation through the example of a lightbulb. If you take a lightbulb and examine it, you can see what a great invention it is. It is made perfectly, but it is useless if not lit up. I mean, what can you do with it without it being connected to the source—electricity? It is good for nothing, but once it is connected and turned on, it serves a great purpose. It brings light to the darkness and helps us to see beyond. It brings clarity into a dark place.

We were designed in the same way. Jesus said, "You are the light of the world" (Matthew 5:14). We are supposed to be the light—not just the lightbulb. Many Christians claim to be the light, but if they are not turned on, then they are useless. They are merely lightbulbs, not bringing clarity into their environment.

If I took a lightbulb and placed it in a box, what would happen? If I brought a lightbulb into a room and placed it alongside other lightbulbs, what good would it be? Unless it is turned on and actually releases light, it will just blend in with the others. Sadly, that is like many so-called Christians who are nothing more than ineffective lightbulbs that give off no light.

But as John said, "Whoever abides in Him does not sin. Whoever sins has neither seen Him nor known Him. . . . Let no one deceive you. He who practices righteousness is righteous. . . . He who sins is of the devil. . . . Whoever has been born of God does not sin" (1 John 3:6–9).

I love Christmas lights. Because they are on a continuous line, they share the same source of power. When one is on, they all are on; when one is out, all of them are out. We need the same source in our lives—we need God. We need to know Him so that we can share Him with others.

One time when my daughter was acting up, I asked her if she knew God. I mean, all she had known for all her young life was God. She prayed, sang, and worshiped the Lord every day, and she went to church, but do you know what her answer was? Her answer was nothing but silence. There was no response whatsoever.

That told me she was neutral. What do I mean by that? Well, she knew Him because I know Him, but maybe she did not know

Him personally. God was teaching me a great lesson. We cannot assume that just because we take our kids to church that they know God or have developed a personal relationship with Him.

Yes, we need to go to work and teach them about God, but first we need to know God for ourselves. We cannot give what we don't have. If you are a "turned on" lightbulb, darkness will still come your way, but because you are connected to the source, it will not affect you. Darkness, when it faces the light, will disappear.

The Smartphone

Let's move now from the analogy of a lightbulb to the analogy of a smartphone. Smartphones are a great invention. I mean, wow, smartphones can do almost anything. They can research, show you pictures, and calculate. They are equipped with the time, a navigation system, and storage capacity, and they even have voice command. But yet they are so dumb. Yes, dumb. A smartphone needs you to operate it, right? Sitting alone, it cannot do a thing. It needs your input to work; without a human mind and hands operating it, it cannot do a thing.

We humans are the same way. We have been designed with talents, abilities, and gifts. We are capable of so much, yet we have not discovered our potential. We cannot discover our fullest potential until we completely surrender to God and receive direction from Him. Only then will we be useful, as the smartphone is when it is in our hands and being directed by us.

Who other than the maker of the smartphone to know exactly what it is made of and what capabilities it has built in to it? I love what Billy Graham wrote in his book *The Reason for My Hope—Salvation*. He said, "Your soul belongs to God. He is the only one who can redeem your soul. It is God who made your soul. It is the Lord Jesus who died to redeem your soul. And it is the Holy Spirit who can fill your soul with God's love and guide you through life. This is the way to have victory over sin." [page 45] That is what separates us from the world's system.

CHAPTER 13

Cast of Characters

God said, "Be holy because I am holy." Our call is to be just that. It is a command—a direct command and a personal command—when He says to be holy. If we are to represent God, we need to live a pure and holy life—not perfect, but holy. One of several definitions of the word *holy* means "to be separated to" or "to be separated from." It means to live separated or consecrated to God and separated from the world's values.

In the Bible, we learn that Enoch walked with God, and his reward was heaven. Elijah, as we learned from previous chapters, served the Lord and lived a holy life. As a result, he went straight to heaven. Moses, after his reencounter with God in the burning bush, was purified and devoted himself to serving and walking with God. Denying himself, his pleasures, his entire life, he lived serving God and serving others.

Joshua followed in the same footsteps as Moses. He obeyed God, living a pure life full of knowledge. He was filled with the Spirit and the Word of God, meditating on it day and night.

Joshua

From his mentor, Moses, Joshua learned all about God. He experienced, lived, and saw all the miracles God did through Moses. He was a faithful, respectful follower with strong character and a firm demeanor. He stood steadfast with Moses. Perhaps he learned that one day he would take Moses' place, or perhaps the thought did not occur to him that one day he would replace God's anointed, faithful servant. Regardless, he was a young, strong, mighty man of valor. He understood life and, most importantly, the giver of life. He developed his calling and did his job accordingly—faithfully, honestly, and with integrity.

One day, God Himself—not his father Nun or his mentor Moses—spoke to Joshua and told him that because Moses was now dead, Joshua would lead God's people to the Promised Land. Through the knowledge and leadership of this new faithful servant, God would manifest Himself to direct the twelve tribes of Israel as they headed to the Promised Land flowing with milk and honey. It was through the servanthood of Joshua that God would deliver His promise to His chosen people.

The Lord instructed the young man in the way he should go, and that was righteous and holy, calling him to be strong and courageous. God commanded Joshua to read the Word and meditate on it day and night, and He promised him that just as He had been with Moses, so would He be with him. He told him only to be strong and courageous, and if he followed God's commands, he would have great success in all he did.

I believe that the eyes of the Lord were set on this fine young man, who had proven himself over and over to be someone worthy, someone who had separated himself to obey and serve his Creator. Joshua was someone who had seen the glory of God, and God was the only thing on his mind and soul. He had seen that there is no other way, and he knew that there was only one God, the God of gods, the creator God of all things—Elohim.

Not all of Joshua's generation made it to the Promised Land. Most of them were left in the desert because of their disobedience and wrongdoing. Joshua and Caleb were the only ones spared; for being obedient to God's calling, they were allowed to enter the Promised Land. Through the years, they had been obedient to His commands, obedient to His voice, obedient to walk a holy walk in His presence.

Just like Moses, Joshua did not have time to monkey around. He had no time to waste— no time to be a Don Juan or tattoo his body or pierce his ears. He understood that his body was not his, but the temple of the living God. He understood that he needed to keep his body clean, pure, and holy for God alone.

Joshua only had time to focus on his prize and reward—his heavenly reward. He denied himself and served the Lord, seeking first God's kingdom and not his own. He understood that his purpose in life was to love the Lord God with all his heart, mind, and soul; to walk in His ways; to keep His ways; to keep His commands; to hold fast to Him; and to serve Him with all his heart and with all his soul (Joshua 22:5). He did an exceptional job of it.

"How was Joshua able to listen to the Lord?" you might ask. Well, he had developed a pure heart. Jesus said that the ones with pure hearts will see God, and the ones who know Him will hear His voice.

Now, to you—not your mom, dad, or anyone else in your family—the Lord Jesus Himself says, "Anyone who intends to come with me has to let me lead. You're not in the driver's seat; *I* am. Don't run from suffering; embrace it. Follow me and I'll show you how. Self-help is no help at all. Self-sacrifice is the way, my way, to finding yourself, your true self. What kind of deal is it to get everything you want but lose yourself? What could you ever trade your soul for?" (Matthew 16:24–26 MSG). Are you up to that challenge?

Are you ready to live a new life, a blessed life? This is a life in which you may not see an earthly reward, but you are storing up a heavenly one. This kind of life—a life of self-denial, an "unpopularity" contest that is different from normal, everyday life—is not very common in the world today.

Not to his mom, not to his dad, but to Joshua himself did God come, informing him that Moses was dead and that he was the one chosen to deliver the people into the Promised Land.

Esther

In the Bible, we see that God calls not only men to do His will, but also women. There are many examples in the Bible of women who took their sandals off their feet. Esther comprehended and followed instructions the way they were outlined for her. She was given the opportunity to go before the king, but to do so, she needed to be completely purified so she could find favor with him. She thus decided to purify herself with myrrh for six months before she ever approached the king. She understood that she was called to deliver God's people, her nation. She understood that she needed to take off her sandals and be completely clean if she was to serve the Lord God through an earthly king. The reward was that she was used to bring glory to God, save lives, save communities, save cities, and save nations. In the same way, we need to daily come clean and purify ourselves before God.

If we look closely at all the prophets and all God's anointed people, we see that God used them to deliver a person, a community, or the children of His promise. We can see it in the stories of Noah, Abraham, Jacob, Joseph, Moses, Joshua, Gideon, and Jonah, among others. They were all called, not to build their own empires, but to be molded, prepared, and empowered to deliver a family, a community, a village, or a nation. They had to remove theirs sandals completely because the ground where they were standing or was about to enter was holy. Every time God's people stood on holy ground in His service, they won the battle. Apart from it, they were defeated by their opponents. Similarly, every time we serve in the name of the Lord, we are walking on holy ground. Everywhere we go in His name, we are walking on holy ground.

In God's Service

You must understand that holy ground is not only when you are in His presence— talking, praying, or worshiping the Lord—but every time you are at His service, whether preaching, teaching, ministering, counseling, worshiping, singing, or so forth. Every time you are sharing His love, His forgiveness, His grace, or His mysteries, you are standing on holy ground. Every time you are praying for others, giving, helping in His great name, you are standing on holy ground. If you weren't, He wouldn't be there to give and overshadow you, working His miracles through you just like He did with Moses. Every time Moses did something miraculous, he did it because the presence of God was with Him. Moses was standing and walking on holy ground all the years he served God.

When God sends you somewhere, you will be empowered and protected. He will guide you and will win the battle through you and for you. Your reward is eternal life in the mansion He has prepared for you. As 1 Samuel 2:8–9 says, "He raises the poor from the dust and lifts the beggar from the ash heap, to set them among princes and make them inherit the throne of glory. For the pillars of the earth are the LORD's, and He has set the world upon them. He will guard the feet of His saints, but the wicked shall be silent in darkness. For by strength no man shall prevail."

Also, Ecclesiastes 5:1 exhorts us, "Walk prudently when you go to the house of God; and draw near to hear rather than to give the sacrifice of fools, for they do not know that they do evil."

CHAPTER 14

When Your Call Comes

For many followers of truth, or for many who have the desire of servanthood, the question most often asked is, "How will I know when God calls?" In my journey, that was the question I asked myself over and over again. I even asked other leaders and ministers about it. They did not go into a lot of detail with me but just said, "When the time comes, you will know it."

You may feel that you need to start doing things on your own, but it is God who prepares you, molds you, shapes you. It is God who chooses you and calls you to His ministry. It is He who exalts you or promotes you in His time.

In the story of Samuel, Samuel was delivered to serve at the temple in his early years. The priest, Eli at the time, guided and mentored the young prophet-in-the making. The Bible tells us that in those days, the revelation of God was rarely heard or seen. God was distant from the people until He decided to call Samuel to lead His people.

We all need an Eli in our childhood, in our adolescence, and even in our adulthood to lead us to the Lord. Once connected, we need to follow and listen to the voice of the Lord, for He is the one who calls and the one who develops that relationship with us. When God called Samuel, Eli was there, directing him to God.

The Bible tells us that although the boy Samuel ministered in the temple, he did not know God for himself. Before the revelation of God was given to him personally, Samuel did not know how God would talk to him. He knew of the Lord, but he did not know the Lord on a personal level (1 Samuel 3:7).

This happens to all of us. We know of God, but do not know Him. We might even be serving God, yet He has not been revealed to us personally. There is a big difference between knowing of God and knowing Him personally. When God finally called Samuel, it was a pure encounter with the living God. It was an encounter that transformed his life forever. From that moment on, Samuel separated himself to live for and serve God and God alone. Samuel definitely took his sandals off his young feet to walk the talk guided and empowered by God.

The Result of Obedience: Joseph

In Egypt, "Joseph said to his brethren, 'I am dying; but God will surely visit you, and bring you out of this land to the land of which He swore to Abraham, to Isaac, and to Jacob.' Then Joseph took an oath from the children of Israel, saying, 'God will surely visit you, and you shall carry up my bones from here.' So Joseph died, being one hundred and ten years old; and they embalmed him, and he was put in a coffin in Egypt" (Genesis 50:24–26).

Why did Joseph boldly proclaim the coming of God to set His people free? I believe it was simply that Joseph knew the Lord

God and was connected to Him in both the good times and the bad. In the morning and at night, every hour, every minute, every second, every instant, he knew God.

When you understand God and have a close relationship with Him, He will tell you things to come in a dream, in His Word, or even personally, like He did with Abraham. When He was ready to destroy the cities of Sodom and Gomorrah, God said to Abraham:

> "Shall I hide from Abraham what I am doing, since Abraham shall surely become a great and mighty nation, and all the nations of the earth shall be blessed in him? For I have known him, in order that he may command his children and his household after him, that they keep the way of the Lord, to do righteousness and justice, that the Lord may bring to Abraham what He has spoken to him." And the Lord said, "Because the outcry against Sodom and Gomorrah is great, and because their sin is very grave, I will go down now and see whether they have done altogether according to the outcry against it that has come to Me; and if not, I will know."
>
> Genesis 18:17–21

The same way that God had communicated with Abraham, He communicated with Joseph. Joseph was given spiritual eyes; he had the faith and certainty that God was coming to visit His people and set them free from that foreign land. Joseph even asked that his bones be transferred to the Promised Land they were about to receive. Joseph knew for sure that the Lord God was coming to set them free from the hands of Pharaoh. His brothers, however, could not understand that coming event, even if Joseph had tried to convince them.

All who are walking with the Lord today, all those who are following Him, have the same assurance that the Lord God is coming back a second time to set us free. This time, however, it will not be to rescue us from Pharaoh's hand, but to deliver us from the evil one, Satan, as He brings us to the promised place He has prepared—eternal life with Him in heaven.

Jacob's call came one-on-one with the Angel of the Lord when he wrestled with Him.

Joseph's call came through dreams.

Moses' call came through the burning bush.

Joshua's call came from God Himself.

Elisha's call came from a messenger of God, Elijah.

David's call came by way of a prophet, Samuel.

The twelve apostles' call came directly from the Lord Jesus Christ.

Paul's call came through a heavenly light shining around him—Jesus Himself.

Your call might not come through the sky, a burning bush, or a light shining from the sky. Your call will come when you are ready. It will come when God approves it.

I remember my call came after I surrendered all to God. It came when I decided to live for Him and only Him.

How about you? Are you waiting for your call? Has your call come yet?

Your Anointing

Someone has said that the anointing is in the marketplace, not just on the platform. Jesus carried the cross on a street, not in a church. The anointing is in your talent and ability. David was not anointed to be a prophet, preacher, or priest, but rather, he was anointed to be a king. Peter was anointed to be an evangelist. Paul was anointed to be a teacher. Elisha was anointed to be a prophet.

What is your anointing? Whatever it is, your anointing is just for you. When Samuel went to anoint a new king as the Lord directed, he at first thought one of Jesse's older sons must be the one God had chosen. However, the anointing was not for the firstborn or one of the older sons, as Samuel thought it would be. The anointing was directed and chosen by God alone.

God looks on the inside; He looks at a man's heart. This is what He told Samuel when He directed him to anoint David, Jesse's youngest son, as king. Men look at appearances, at the outside, but God looks at the inside. It doesn't matter where you are today. Your anointing will come just where you are. Remember, David was a shepherd working in the pastures when his anointing came. Elisha was working the fields when his anointing came. You will be anointed in the marketplace where you are. Whether that is on the football field, baseball field, corn field, or any other field, just shine for God.

What is your anointing?

CHAPTER 15

His Ways, Not Mine

When you do not know God, you fall for anything. As a young person, when you just know of God versus knowing Him personally, you will listen to your peers and do what your friends dare you to do. Why? It is because you want to prove to them that you are in full control. You want to prove that any decisions you make, good or bad, are indeed your own decisions, not your mom's, not your dad's, and certainly not God's.

When you don't know God, you will tattoo your body, even though the Bible instructs us not to do that in Exodus 19. You will also pierce your body, even though we were instructed not to do that either. You will get drunk, you will disrespect your parents, and you will lie, rob, and steal, among other bad things. The fear of the Lord is not within you.

What is the fear of the Lord? Proverbs 1:7 declares, "The fear of the Lord is the beginning of knowledge, but fools despise wisdom and instruction." Until we understand who God really is and develop a reverential fear of Him, we cannot possess true wisdom. True wisdom comes only from understanding who God is and recognizing that He is holy, just, and righteous.

Someone once said, "The fear of the Lord is an awareness that you are in the presence of a holy, just, and almighty God and that He will hold you accountable for your motives, thoughts, words, and actions. To fear God is to desire to live in harmony with His righteous standards and to honor Him in all that you do."

Jesus' disciples, before they reencountered the resurrected King, were living according to the world's standards. They were lying, denying, betraying and doing other such things. But once they encountered Jesus face-to-face after His resurrection, they understood His ways and His kingdom. Their lives were forever transformed.

Anyone can call himself a Christian, and it is good to identify yourself as one, but that is not enough. You must act like one and live like one as well. You must imitate Him and the high standards He set. "Follow me," He says, "and do My will." Second Timothy 2:19 declares that "God's solid foundation stands firm, sealed with this inscription: 'The Lord knows those who are his,' and, 'Everyone who confesses the name of the Lord must turn away from wickedness'" (NIV).

I was helping out at a church event, and there was a new man volunteering. We were introduced by the person in charge of the ministry, and I discovered he had been sent to shadow me so he could learn how to help, pray, and lead people in need. We got to talking, building rapport. Since he was a thirty-seven-year-old man, I figured he might have a family, so I asked him, "Are you married?" to which he answered, "No, I'm not. "Looking carefully at me, he then added, "I'm not married because I'm a homosexual."

I was surprised, because he looked quite masculine and his way of talking was straight. He was not like other homosexuals

I'd met, whose speech and mannerisms were more feminine. Now I'm not condemning homosexuals; every one of us has hang-ups and issues we need to overcome. For some, it might be homosexuality, while for others, it might be adultery, fornication, pornography, anger, drug use, or any number of things. We all have a sickness that we need to be healed of. We are all sinners who need a redeemer. We need a Savior—we need Christ. We need to take our shoes off our feet and walk in holiness in all our actions and doings, especially when we are serving in the name of the Lord.

I told this man, "There is nothing that the blood of Jesus cannot change. In Jesus, we become new. We have been given new life in Him." Friends, if you don't like the life you are living, get a new one! Be born again and start fresh.

I'm not going to draw any conclusions about this person. I will leave it up to you to do that. But what do you think about this case? There are many people like him serving in our churches. If a homosexual goes to church and accepts Christ but continues to practice sin, would you call him a homosexual Christian? There is no such thing. If a crooked businessman calls himself a Christian but doesn't change, does he then become a dishonest Christian? Does a man living in adultery who calls himself a Christian become an adulterous Christian? What do you think about that?

Just putting a Christian label on a person doesn't make that person a Christian. Just because you go to or serve at church doesn't make you one either. You don't become a car just because you spend a lot of time in the garage. You can even sleep in the garage, but it will not make you a car. Christians are known by their reflection of God and their imitation of their model, Jesus Christ.

How to Know God

How can you know if you truly know God? It's when you obey Him—when you not only read the Bible, but also start to do what it says; when you listen to your spirit and do what it's prompting you to do. When you obey God, you are no longer like a stubborn son who is always looking for ways to do what he wants. Live knowing that you have a heavenly Father who loves you and walks with you, a Father who longs to communicate with you and give you the desires of your heart. At your reencounter with Christ, you'll know for certain that you have come to know God.

Do you feel that perhaps you know God, but you are not quite certain about it? When Jacob was running away from his brother to the land of Nahor, he went to sleep one night and had a dream. He saw a stairway touching earth and leading up to heaven, and he watched angels going up and down it:

> Then GOD was right before him, saying, "I am GOD, the God of Abraham your father and the God of Isaac. I'm giving the ground on which you are sleeping to you and to your descendants. Your descendants will be as the dust of the Earth; they'll stretch from west to east and from north to south. All the families of the Earth will bless themselves in you and your descendants. Yes. I'll stay with you, I'll protect you wherever you go, and I'll bring you back to this very ground. I'll stick with you until I've done everything I promised you."
>
> Jacob woke up from his sleep. He said, "God is in this place—truly. And I didn't even know it!" He was terrified.

He whispered in awe, "Incredible. Wonderful. Holy. This is God's House. This is the Gate of Heaven."

Genesis 28:13–17 MSG

After this encounter, Jacob knew God and promised to give Him 10 percent of all his earnings, before he had ever earned any (verses 20–22).

According to the Bible, Job was a blameless and upright man who respected God and kept far from sin and evil. But after a time of suffering, hardship, and questioning God, he said, "I have heard of You by the hearing of the ear, but now my eye sees You" (Job 42:5).

In other words, before Job knew God personally, he was like so many of us who know of God only through other people, the books and articles we read, and so on. However, we have not had an encounter with Him. We may even acknowledge Him, try to obey Him, and work hard at keeping our lives blameless and upright. But when we look more closely, we realize that all our knowledge of Him is superficial. Suddenly, at a reencounter with Him, our eyes are opened, and we see the glory of God for ourselves.

How wonderful life becomes when we truly know that God is real and alive, when we know beyond a shadow of a doubt that He is always there. After Balaam's donkey saw the Angel of the Lord, the prophet too was eventually able to see the glory of God. He cried out to heaven, realizing that God was real and always with him.

Some people pray as if there might be a God, while others pray because they know there is one. Which are you?

CHAPTER 16

Heaven, Our Final Destination

If heaven is your final destination, how are you doing on your journey there? We all know that we will get to heaven, not by works or by being a good person, but by God's Son, Jesus Christ. He is the only road to heaven. How is your relationship with Him? That relationship will determine how close or how far you are from your final destination.

Fast check: God wants us to love the Lord our God with all of our hearts, all of our minds, and all of our strength. How are you doing with that? He also said that we need to love our neighbors as we love ourselves. How is your love for others? The Lord summed up all the Ten Commandments in these two commands. He made it simple for us to understand.

Examine Yourself

"But let a man examine himself," says 1 Corinthians 11:28. There is no man or woman who can point a finger at you. Only you can do that. If you are in Christ, not even God judges you, but gives you grace and free will. But who better than you to determine where you are in the ways of God? Only you know how your life truly is. People see only your outer appearance, but only you know the interior workings of your heart.

Can you fool someone about your heart or inner condition? Absolutely! But you can never fool God. He knows you inside and out. Remember, He made you, calls you by name, and even has the hairs of your head numbered. He is your dad, and that is why you can cry, "Abba, Father!"

So why keep contemplating and holding on to all the bad things you have done? If you do that, all you do is delay what God has already prepared for you. God cannot send you to the next level when you have not yet passed or mastered the first. You cannot go to second grade if you have not yet passed first grade. You cannot go to home base until you have walked or run through the other three bases.

Come clean with God. Go to the well and be purified with the living water.

Your Final Destination

When your last breath escapes from your body, it's all over. All the things you put off for another time will be left undone. There is no more time to do what you didn't do, and there is no more time to repent and to forgive.

All your possessions stay here as well. You do not take a single thing with you. The next thing you know, you are at the judgment seat of Christ to receive either your salvation or your condemnation. You will hear pronounced over you, "Well done, good and faithful servant," or "You wicked and lazy servant" (Matthew 25:21, 26).

In the year 1992, I did not know much about God and His mysteries. One day a coworker said to me, "Rob, do you know that if I were to die today, I know where I'm going? I'm going to heaven!"

I looked at him as if he had three eyes on his forehead. I did not understand what he was saying and thought he was crazy. I didn't know how to respond, so I didn't say a word. He continued to tell me all the wonders of God, how He loves us and gives us opportunities to get to know Him on a personal level. He told me that I had an opportunity to be cleansed of all my sins and become a new person in Him if I would only accept Him in my heart and follow Him. He shared what God had done in his life, but I could not relate to what he was saying because I was naive about the Word of God and the mysteries of the Lord.

The following morning, he continued the talk and said, "You know, I had a conversation with Jesus on the way to work today. I felt as if He were sitting right there in the car with me."

I looked at him and thought to myself, *Wow, this man has been smoking the real thing today!* Remembering our conversation from the previous day, I could not understand how he could know beforehand his final destination.

A few years later, after I had come to know God and His mysteries, I realized that this person was not joking. All that "nonsense" he had shared with me was indeed real. God's Word verified everything he said; and if God's Word says it, it is true. As I shared in chapter 10, if we confess with our mouth that Jesus is the way, and if we follow His ways and live accordingly, we secure our way to heaven through Him.

As long as we are alive, we have the choice of where we will spend eternity. My walk with the Lord began in 1995 when I confessed and received Him as my Lord and Savior. Later, in 2011, I came to know the Lord on a deeper, more personal level. That is when I had my reencounter with Him. That changed my life forever.

A year later, I traveled out of state to visit my parents. I began sharing Jesus with them, saying, "Mom, Dad, this is not going to make sense to you, and I know that you are going to think I'm crazy, but this is what the Lord says." Then I began to tell them what I had learned, and I shared with them my personal experiences with God. They reacted exactly the way I had reacted when my coworker shared his relationship with the Lord with me. I saw the unbelief on their faces, and they looked at me as if I were crazy and on drugs.

I knew they were going to react the same way I had when I first heard about heaven and earth. That was okay with me, because the one thing I knew was that they could sense and see the difference in me. Praising and glorifying my Lord and Savior Jesus Christ was all that mattered to me. Three days later, my parents re committed their lives to the Lord Jesus Christ. Praise to the Lord!

This was an experience I will never forget. I was a channel for my parents to come to God and begin a new friendship with Christ. For them, God had always been just a story, just like it had been for me so many years earlier; but that day, God became real to them. For my mom and dad, that day marked the beginning of a new life in a relationship with the Lord our God. They now had a personal relationship with the Lord, whereas before, they had only an empty form of religion that was taking them nowhere.

Well Done, Good and Faithful Servant

After your journey on earth is over and you have completed your daily walk in His presence without your sandals on, you reach the finish line. Like with everything else in life, after you finish the race, God has your reward ready for you. Throughout your walk on earth, you sometimes may have thought about those great words of affirmation that He would personally say to you. You probably had some moments when you checked yourself to see if you were on the right track, making adjustments as needed. But you were full of God's grace, and because of it, you were assured that you were indeed on the right path.

Finally, you make it to the finish line, and there God the Father is waiting for you. He is proud of you, telling His angels about you, bestowing upon you a crown of glory, the crown of eternal life. This is the crown that only He can provide, and after receiving it, you hear those sweet and joyful words: "Well done, good and faithful servant; you were faithful over a few things, I will make you ruler over many things. Enter into the joy of your lord" (Matthew 25:21).

Wow, you enter into His joy and feel so light. You are given a new body; all the aching you felt on your earthly journey is gone. All the worries, disappointments, and tears of heartache have all disappeared too. You have entered into eternal life with great rewards.

I Never Knew You

Again, life is full of choices. Hopefully, we make the right ones and are rewarded with the crown of life. But what if we decide to follow our own way and live according to our own understanding? And what if this is a path that is contrary to holiness and His ways of living?

Chip Ingram came out with a new book called *True Spirituality—Becoming a Romans 12 Christian*. In it, he zeroes in on the teaching in Romans 12:1–2: "I urge you, brothers and sisters, in view of God's mercy, to offer your bodies as a living sacrifice, holy and pleasing to God—this is your true and proper worship. Do not conform to the pattern of this world, but be transformed by the renewing of your mind. Then you will be able to test and approve what God's will is—his good, pleasing and perfect will" (NIV).

Chip's whole platform is teaching us to do and not just say. However, in today's society, there is much talk but little walk. The world's standard is even in the church. Statistically, the divorce rate is over 50 percent, both in the world and in the church, and statistics on other issues reflect the same trend. As someone has said, "There are so many churches in the world today, and so much of the world in the church."

One day I was attending a men's meeting at a local church with over five hundred men in attendance. There were games, refreshments, and music. You might have thought that the music being played would be Christian music, but no, it was the same music that the world plays. I stood there, listening and looking around. There is nothing wrong with having some fun, but the extreme loudness and worldliness of the music made me feel as if I were in the temple when Jesus cleansed it of the moneychangers.

Yes, we might be serving in the temple, but do we do as Romans 12:1–2 recommends? Do we offer our bodies as living sacrifices, pleasing God rather than men, not conforming to the world but being transformed by the renewing of our minds? God wants us to be holy; that is, separated to Him and separated from the world. We must be separated from the world's system, a system that calls *good* bad and *bad* good. The world's system is ruled by evil, and many so-called brothers are part of it without even knowing it. Our sandals must always be off when we walk on holy ground.

I think Psalm 99:6–9 says it well: "Moses and Aaron were among his priests, Samuel was among those who called on his name; they called on the LORD and he answered them. He spoke to them from the pillar of cloud; they kept his statutes and the decrees he gave them. LORD our God, you answered them; you were to Israel a forgiving God, though you punished their misdeeds. Exalt the LORD our God and worship at his holy mountain, for the Lord our God is holy" (NIV).

Jesus is the way, the truth, and the life. All He has taught us is true. At our final destination, we will receive either the crown of life or eternal punishment—a ticket to the lake of fire. His sober warning to all those who do not walk in His ways is, "Not everyone who says to Me, 'Lord, Lord,' shall enter the kingdom of heaven, but he who does the will of My Father in heaven. Many will say to Me in that day, 'Lord, Lord, have we not prophesied in Your name, cast out demons in Your name, and done many wonders in Your name?' And then I will declare to them, 'I never knew you; depart from Me, you who practice lawlessness!'" (Matthew 7:21–23).

If you are on the right track but not walking in the way that He commands, you will suffer the consequences. Instead, present your body as a living sacrifice. Sell out to God completely, walk in His ways, and take the sandals off your feet. Then you will have no fear of missing your eternal reward.

CHAPTER 17

What Is Expected of Me?

God expects us to know the Word, but better yet, He expects us to obey it. As His Word says, obedience is better than sacrifice. We can't just quote Scripture and not do what it asks of us. Anyone can quote Scripture, as many recordings demonstrate.

I learned this lesson well one evening when my wife was helping my daughter with her homework. My daughter was memorizing some words for her social studies class, and my wife asked her, "Do you know what those words mean?" My daughter, who was eleven years old at the time, responded, "Not really."

My wife continued, saying, "You need to not only memorize these words, but also to understand their meanings so that you will know what you are doing." Then she added, "It is so important to understand their meanings rather than just memorizing them."

My wife then began to teach our daughter the meanings of the words. After that, my daughter was better able to comprehend what she was studying. As the words became alive with meaning, she now understood more fully. Because my wife taught her with pictures and examples, she could see the picture clearly.

So many times we just say things—even the words of Scripture—failing to grasp the importance and the meaning of them.

"Inherited" Christianity

Besides just talking but not walking the walk, many people merely put on Christian ID tags and think that by doing so, they are automatically one. However, in these same people is no change, no transformation. Yes, they are labeled "Christian," but their actions say otherwise. I'm not judging—just being honest and sharing some of the things I myself did before I knew better.

We see many examples of this in the Bible and in everyday life. For example, in the Bible, we read that even though Eli served God in his capacity as high priest, his sons were corrupt and did not know the Lord (1 Samuel 2:12). They committed grievous sins against God. Samuel's sons did not follow in the footsteps of their father, who served the Lord in truth and obedience. In 1 Samuel 8:3–5, we read:

> His sons did not walk in his ways; they turned aside after dishonest gain, took bribes, and perverted justice.
>
> Then all the elders of Israel gathered together and came to Samuel at Ramah, and said to him, "Look, you are old, and your sons do not walk in your ways. Now make us a king to judge us like all the nations."

Today there are many families—even preachers' families—facing the same situation. The kids are living totally the opposite from their parents. They may wear the Christian tag, but they are following the ways of the world—drinking, marrying, divorcing, piercing their ears, tattooing their bodies, lying, jealousy. They live in darkness rather than in the light.

Don't just carry a Christian label, but be a true follower of truth and a doer of the Word, living as a child of the most high God.

Willingness

My wife and I have taught our daughter that to follow Christ is voluntary, and we have explained to her that God does not force us to love Him or to follow Him. Neither does He force us to pray to Him. We have told our daughter that we will not force her to follow God. If she follows Him or calls herself a Christian just because her parents do, that will not work. Maybe she could fool herself, but others would know the truth, because true Christians are known by their actions. Anyone can put on the Christian tag, but it doesn't mean it is true.

To be a true Christian requires willingness, a personal choice to be like Him, to walk like Him, to serve like Him, to talk like Him. It means we imitate Christ, teaching like Him, obeying like Him, suffering like Him, living like Him. When Jesus was about to be delivered up for crucifixion, He prayed, "Father, if it is Your will, take this cup away from Me; nevertheless not My will, but Yours, be done" (Luke 22:42). We can do no less.

That is total submission, taking your sandals off your feet because you have stepped onto holy ground. You are standing on ground that is not yours, but rather belongs to your Father God.

The Rules

The Ten Commandments are rules of conduct, but they do not identify us as children of God. They are simply rules of conduct that indicate our level of commitment to God's standards of holiness. However, they are important, and when we disobey them, we will reap the consequences that come as a result of our disobedience.

Made of Dust

Who are we to disobey God's mandate? We were made for Him and through Him, so who are we to question our maker? Though we are but dust, we have been given Jesus, the breath of life. That breath of life sustains us, holds us together, and guides us towards our heavenly Father.

The first time I read Isaiah 41:14, I paused and considered what I had just read. The Lord God referred to Jacob as "worm Jacob." I could not understand this, especially since in the preceding verse, He had just said, "For I, the LORD your God, will hold your right hand, saying to you, 'Fear not, I will help you'" (verse 13). It seemed like such a swift change in tone.

We need to understand that God is God and we are not. We are just dust, created into being by His powerful and marvelous hand. As soon as He formed us, He blew spirit into us, making us living beings.

God is powerful, tender, loving, and kind. He holds everything together—from the waters, to the stars, to the grass, to the heavens. We are nothing compared to Him. Don't get me wrong. Yes, He loves us and wants the best for us. We were created in His image; in the image of God, we were created male and female. He gave mankind authority over all His creation, even giving us power to multiply ourselves and give life to others in the form of our own image. We were given the ability to reproduce—not create, but duplicate.

God's Word is perfect, and His promises are real and true. On our journey to growing in holiness before Him, He promises that He will always be with us. He knows that without Him, we are nothing, but in Him, we are whole. We need to realize that without Him we are just worms, which one online source defines as a weak or despicable person.

If you observe physical worms, you will notice that they come out of the soil when it rains. Initially, you will see them moving about; but minutes later they are dry, and a few hours later they turn to dust. Why? They were disconnected from the soil, their source of life and nutrition. Similarly, we must remain on the Vine if we are to stay connected to our source, God.

The Need to Be Connected

God's purpose in making us was so that we could be with Him always. He wanted us to be connected to Him. Think about it. After creating everything else, He made us humans. We cannot boast that we were involved in the creation, because we definitely were not. He made Adam first, then Eve, and joined them in holy matrimony. Genesis 2:22 records the first bride ever to walk the aisle, with her Father uniting her to Adam in holy matrimony. The first marriage was created and performed by the

Creator Himself—God Almighty. God taught the first married couple one of the greatest mysteries of mankind, the mystery of living as one flesh.

God loved man's company, but after their fall, everything changed. The land was cursed because of their disobedience, and they distanced themselves from God. The reality of death and deceit started right then in the Garden of Eden. In fact, death made its first appearance when Adam and Eve's oldest son, Cain, killed his younger brother, Abel. You might be asking yourself why God permitted that horrible scene to unfold right at the beginning of time. He did not; the land was cursed after the fall, and the devil was loose and at hand. Cain listened to him and did what he suggested.

The devil came to lie, kill, and destroy. We can very well see that in the Garden of Eden as well as right now. Ever since the fall, the world has been mired in deceit from the evil one. Even Jesus was tempted by Satan, but of course, He resisted temptation, and the tempter fled from Him.

God made us and gave us life. He wants us to live. Note that Adam lived more than 900 years. Wow, can you believe that he lived nearly 1,000 years? As time passed, however, our days on earth diminished. For instance, Noah lived more than 600 years, but Enoch, the one God took to heaven, lived only 365 years. Abraham lived to 175, and Moses lived only to 120. God revealed to Moses in Psalm 90:10 that our years now are only to 70, but if we take care of ourselves, we can live a little past that mark.

God's intention was not for us to perish, but to always be with Him in communion and fellowship. The Lamb was sent as atonement for the fall, to pay the price for our transgressions and sins. He came to show us the way to the Father, and to give us eternal life with God as originally intended.

Every disobedient act separates us from God. In fact, if we disobey or fail to do God's commands, we are not His, but are of the devil. That is why Jesus said, "You are of your father the devil, and the desires of your father you want to do. He was a murderer from the beginning, and does not stand in the truth, because there is no truth in him. When he speaks a lie, he speaks from his own resources, for he is a liar and the father of it" (John 8:44).

Humbleness

Webster's Dictionary defines humbleness as follows: "Reflecting, expressing, or offered in a spirit of deference or submission."

There is divine power when you humble yourself. To humble yourself means to present yourself before God in absolute surrender. You have repented of all your sins and disobedient acts and have asked God to forgive you. You have recognized that He is in full control of all things. You have acknowledged that He is the God of the universe—mighty, sovereign, transcendent, holy—and besides Him, there is no other who rules your life.

You have surrendered yourself to Him, recognizing that without Him you are going nowhere, but with Him you are favored. He has made you to be the light and has given you understanding of His Word and mysteries so that you can live by them and share them with others. He has blessed you with power, provision, favor, and abundance. He continually restores your inner and outer beings. He has granted you peace of mind, joy, blessings, and a great mind and a pure heart to know Him, understand Him, and hear His voice. He has completely restored you and made you whole.

If you are a humble person, when you say or do wrong, you admit it and ask for forgiveness. That is why James 5:16 says, "Confess your sins to each other and pray for each other so that you can live together whole and healed" (MSG). When you are right in a matter, you do not boast, but rather, you praise God and give Him the glory.

Humility is not thinking less of your own self-worth, but thinking less of yourself in deference to others. Jesus showed humility when He washed His disciples' feet, when He left His throne to be with us, when He gave His life for all humankind. That is pure humbleness and meekness.

Jesus said, "Blessed are the meek, for they shall inherit the earth" (Matthew 5:5). Meekness is not weakness. *Merriam Webster's Dictionary* defines meekness as follows: "Having or showing a quiet and gentle nature, not wanting to fight or argue with other people."

A good example of this kind of behavior is found in the story of Moses when his sister Miriam and brother Aaron gossiped about him because of the Ethiopian woman whom he had married. Let's read it in Numbers 1:1–8:

> Then Miriam and Aaron spoke against Moses because of the Ethiopian woman whom he had married; for he had married an Ethiopian woman. So they said, "Has the LORD indeed spoken only through Moses? Has He not spoken through us also? And the LORD heard it. (Now the man Moses was very humble, more than all men who were on the face of the earth.)

Suddenly the LORD said to Moses, Aaron, and Miriam, "Come out, you three, to the tabernacle of meeting!" So the three came out. Then the LORD came down in the pillar of cloud and stood in the door of the tabernacle, and called Aaron and Miriam. And they both went forward. Then He said,

> "Hear now My words:
> If there is a prophet among you,
> I, the LORD, make Myself known to him in a vision;
> I speak to him in a dream.
> Not so with My servant Moses;
> He is faithful in all My house.
> I speak with him face to face,
> Even plainly, and not in dark sayings;
> And he sees the form of the LORD.
> Why then were you not afraid
> To speak against My servant Moses?"

The Bible says that Moses was the meekest man in the whole earth and that God spoke to him face-to-face. Because Moses obeyed the commands of the Lord, starting back on the mountain when He ordered him to take his sandals off his feet, Moses continued to walk a holy life in God's presence. Because of it, God was able to communicate with Moses one-on-one, face-to face. The Lord Himself declared that about Moses when He said, "He is faithful in all My house. I speak with him face to face" (verses 7–8).

What an example this story provides of what happens when someone gossips about a true servant of God.

CHAPTER 18

Therefore Go

"Therefore, go and make disciples of all the nations, baptizing them in the name of the Father and the Son and the Holy Spirit. Teach these new disciples to obey all the commands I have given you. And be sure of this: I am with you always, even to the end of the age" (Matthew 28:19–20 NLT). This passage of Scripture is commonly known as the Great Commission. As I mentioned before, it has three parts: (1) Go and make disciples, (2) Baptize them, and (3) Teach them.

To each and every one of us, God has given a commission to fulfill while on this earth. Let's look at some Bible characters who accepted God's call to do something big for His kingdom, and let's start with Moses. He accomplished so much for God that it is truly incredible.

Moses was devoted to God 100 percent. His entire life centered around serving the Lord. I believe Moses had no time for his own recreation; he did not look to have fun for himself in his own circle. I believe that once he got hold of God, he did not want to let Him go. He looked to please God in everything he did, and serving the Lord, to him, was the greatest fun. This was a person who was completely blessed. He had a beautiful wife and children. He had the protection of God as well as the rod of God with which to do miraculous things.

Moses' commission was to lead the Israelites out of the land of Egypt. God was with him every step of the way, and Moses, with God's help and guidance, did an extraordinary job of freeing His people.

We all are wired differently and have different purposes in life. Our purpose might be big or small, significant or insignificant, ordinary or extraordinary. The Lord gives us different messages, businesses, jobs, resources, ministries, families, and assignments. However, the purpose itself and the size of the calling do not matter.

When we receive any assignment in life, we tend to want everything to be perfect. We think that the timing should be perfect, the weather should be perfect, and our clothes should be perfect. We think that our hair must be perfectly in place, our car needs to be new, our apartment should be a house, our small house should be bigger. If we are concentrating on the flesh, then yes, all those things are important. When we concentrate on the details of an assignment, we will not move.

God, however, doesn't look at things from that perspective. God looks at the heart, not at the physical appearance or condition of the individual. When God commanded Moses to go tell Pharaoh to let His people go, Moses just went. Though initially he focused on his human limitations, condition, and incapability, he eventually focused on God's power and fully embraced God's commission. Remember, he was working as a shepherd when he was called, so he probably lacked impressive clothes and transportation. Additionally, he possessed no natural ability as a speaker. All he had was a desire and determination to serve the living God.

On his daily walk with God, all he had was God. His staff and his rod were all that he needed. In a similar way, we need to depend on God solely, trusting in Him to do whatever needs to be done. He will do it supernaturally, for the battles are His and the victories are ours to enjoy.

When we go in response to God's call, we may not have the rod of God, but we have the Word of God, which is more powerful than anything: "For the word of God is living and powerful, and sharper than any two-edged sword, piercing even to the division of soul and spirit, and of joints and marrow, and is a discerner of the thoughts and intents of the heart" (Hebrews 4:12). We just need to learn how to use it.

So Moses, without impressive transportation, clothing, or eloquence of speech, believed in the Lord God, and the Lord worked His wonders through him. As we learned earlier, Moses was always in communion with God, always looking to Him. He devoted much time to prayer, and He obeyed God in the guidance he received from Him. He understood that without the presence of God, he could do nothing.

Many other Bible characters also accepted their God-given commissions. For example, David, when faced with the task of slaying the giant Goliath, had no knowledge or skill in the use of a sword; neither did he wear any armor. All he had was faith and certainty in the Lord his God. Armed with only a slingshot and a stone (the stone was the Rock), he stepped out in faith and defeated the giant.

Joshua defeated Jericho by marching around the city as commanded by the Lord, and by faith, the walls came crashing down.

By faith, Gideon defeated Israel's oppressors with just a few warriors.

Peter, after he was baptized with the Holy Spirit, stood up in faith and boldly proclaimed Jesus. As a result, thousands were saved.

Jesus was the greatest servant of all, always accepting and fulfilling His Father's will. Though the world expected a very different Messiah, one with great riches and military might, Jesus came to the earth as a baby born in humble surroundings.

Even if you are hiding in the belly of a fish, God will find you and deliver you so you can go forth in His name.

Tychicus was Paul's deliverer, distributing Paul's letters to the churches. (see Ephesians 6:21) Your calling, whether big or small, has a tremendous effect on others, but most important of all, it glorifies our creator God.

Your Commission

Your purpose in life may not be to kill a giant with a slingshot, build an ark, or rebuild the walls of Jerusalem. And it certainly isn't to die on a cross for others to live and inherit eternal life. Jesus alone had that calling and fulfilled it perfectly.

Whether it is something big or small, you have your own commission to accomplish. If you don't know your propose in life, all you need to do is come before the Lord and ask Him. He will show you and lead you. God might have given you five talents, or maybe He gave you just one. Regardless, God gives you your talents in order to execute His plan and expand His kingdom. Sadly, many of us fail to realize this and instead use those talents or resources for our own sakes, building our personal kingdoms instead of His.

The story of Joshua is a good example of using talents and abilities to advance God's kingdom. Joshua's commission was to bring the twelve tribes of Israel into their inheritance. Through Him, God would win the battle and deliver the land that He had promised to Abraham and his descendants. Joshua followed God's commands and guidance and stepped accordingly. Just as Moses did, Joshua did not deviate to the left or to the right. He did his job well, expanding God's kingdom, not his own.

Remember how God commanded Joshua to be strong and courageous and also to meditate on His word day and night? The servant Joshua did just that, and the Lord God was with him every step of the way. The Lord fought and won every battle he faced.

Can you imagine what would have happened if Joshua would have deviated even a little from God's command? What if one night when he was going home, one of his pals had invited him to happy hour, to drink a few cold ones? What if they had then found some attractive young woman and decided to have some fun with her? Of course, that did not happen. Joshua was faithful to God and His commands. God Himself had told Joshua to meditate on His word at all times. God knew evil would tempt him, but if Joshua donned his spiritual armor and used the sword of the Spirit, he would be able to withstand any fiery dart thrown at him.

Hey, how about material riches? What if Joshua had gathered for himself material riches for his family and friends? Again, he did not, because Joshua already had it all. He had riches, fame—you name it—but these were not important to him. God's Spirit was with Joshua, and that kept him from deviating from God's will and plan. Joshua understood that his commission was to deliver the goods, and he did.

It doesn't matter what your calling is. All you need to do is to be faithful to God in following His guidance, and you will be blessed on the way.

Your Purpose

When we talk about the characters of the Bible, we always hear about the most famous ones, like King David, Moses, Solomon, Isaiah, and others. As great as those men were, I want to talk to you about someone who is not in the Bible or in anyone's top 10. Nonetheless, this is someone who has separated himself to God, obeying his calling and executing his purpose, and his name is written in the Book of Life.

You are that someone, if you are living for God and have been separated for Him. Not only do you hear His voice, but you obey it as well. You have patiently waited for His calling and have done your best to fulfill it. You were marvelously made, and you have been given a purpose. You may not be fulfilling it yet, because somewhere, somehow that divine connection was severed, and you feel broken and worthless because of the situation you are in. It is normal to feel that way, but not healthy to linger in it. Don't stay in that place, but get up! Seek God, repent, and be water baptized. If you do not like the life you are living, know that God has given you a chance to be born again. Grab hold of that new life with new meaning and new purpose.

In the garden, Adam's purpose as a son of God was to obey God and fellowship with Him, but he disobeyed and suffered the consequences. His communion with God was broken, his purpose was blocked, and he was removed from the presence of God. The same thing that caused him to be distant from God—his disobedience—is what causes us to be distant from God.

Then God sent the second Adam, His beloved Son, who was faithful and obedient to death. What was Jesus's purpose here on earth? It was to obey God the Father and execute God's will. Jesus obeyed God's calling for His life. He was obedient to His calling, His purpose. He glorified God the Father in all things. As He did, God exalted Him, even at Calvary. There Jesus was exalted, put on high for all to see. Everyone there literally had to look up to Him. What evil meant for bad, God turned into good. He is still doing that for you and me.

One Chance

I don't know about you, but as for me, I don't take things lightly. I know that I have only one chance to do things right and live for God. I didn't always know this, however. For thirty-eight years, I saw only my little circle of life. I thought I was responsible only for me and my success. I tried to move mountains on my own, not knowing that all had been given to me. Because I was blind and unaware of the gifts and abilities that had been prepared and placed inside me, I did not move forward.

My understanding of life was horizontal. It was as though I had a compass pointing everywhere but up. Though I wanted to move up in all my endeavors, my compass did not support that. If I were to go up, it was up to me to figure out how to get there, I thought. So I tried and I tried; however, I never amounted to anything great.

I had been in business for many years when one day I took a close look at my life. Many people who had started businesses after me had become successful very quickly. I asked myself why they were more successful than I was, and I wondered whether something was wrong with me. I discovered two problems: (1) I was not applying myself and putting in the work necessary to achieve the level of success I wanted. (2) I believe it was not the will of God for me to be super wealthy or financially successful. I was not wired for business, and maybe I had wrong motives.

You may be asking, "What do you mean, it was not the will of God?" Well, at that time in my life, I was not totally surrendered to the Lord. If God had allowed me to achieve financial success, I would probably have lost it anyway and lost my soul in the process. I learned that where my treasure is, there will my heart be also (Luke 12:34).

That was confirmed from above when I asked God the following question: "God," I said, "why is it that others succeed, but not me?" Two weeks passed without an answer, but one day I was having lunch by myself and meditating on the matter when suddenly God spoke to me. "Picture all the animals," He said.

I began to imagine all kinds of animals—from a cow, to a horse, to a chicken, and so on. I responded, "Okay, I'm visualizing them."

Then He said, "Each and every one of them is different. Each and every one of them serves a purpose."

"Okay," I responded, "that makes sense."

Then He added, "Now picture all the people." I started to visualize all kinds of people, and He added, "Everyone looks the same, but each one has their own purpose."

I answered, "Okay, I can see that." I did not hear Him anymore after that.

I was confused. I didn't understand what He was trying to teach me in that moment. I had expected a clear answer, but all I got was more confusion and more thinking to do. I continued to think on the matter until finally, many days later, I understood what He was trying to say to me.

This is my interpretation of what He taught me: Just like with the animals, we all have a unique design and purpose. A chicken will never do the job of a horse and vice versa, and so it goes with each of the animals. Humankind is the same; each and every one of us has a skill, gift, and purpose in life. If I'm designed to be a contractor, I cannot do the work of a doctor, and so on. Can I learn other trades besides the one I'm good at? Definitely! But it will not be my field of expertise. I am not a salesman, and when I tried to be one, it was hard. I was lousy at it. I never mastered it and thus was never successful in that field. Besides, my heart was too soft when it came to selling. I felt bad making a profit on a product, although it was totally legal, honest, and ethical to do so. I was made for something different.

The apostle Paul was a teacher. He wrote one-third of the New Testament, teaching us the oracles of God. John was a relational person, loving and kind. King David was not a prophet or a teacher, but he was anointed to be a king. Samuel was not separated to be a king or an evangelist, but rather, he was a prophet. How about you? What are you designed for?

I was brought up in a very humble home. I have learned that when you come a long way, you appreciate life more. When you start with nothing and achieve something, you cannot hide your thankfulness and gladness. I might not have earthly riches, but I'm rich. Yes, I'm wealthy! I have peace of mind and a joyful heart. But most importantly, I have a personal relationship with the Son of the creator of the universe. This same Son has given me direct access to God, whom I can call my Father. He is my heavenly Father—the one who loves me, cares for me, guides me, and keeps me—the Father who supplies all my needs.

God told Moses to go. *Go* is an action verb, so Moses was sent to set God's people free from slavery and oppression. God had heard their cries of affliction. When Jesus came to this earth, He commanded us to act on that action word. He also told us to go—to go and make disciples of all nations. In other words, He sent us to set people free from sin, from oppression, and from the world's system. He sent us to go bring them to the light and to teach them to obey and walk in holiness.

Open Invitation

In the Old Testament, God appeared to Moses and told him directly, "Take your sandals off your feet," and he did. Soon after Joshua crossed the Jordan on dry ground, all the males of the second generation of the children of Israel were circumcised. These were the ones who had been born in the wilderness. A relational God always communicates with His children. In the fifth chapter of Joshua, verse 9, we learn that God was preparing His servant for a great commission, saying, "This day I have rolled away the reproach of Egypt from you." One definition of the word *reproach* is something that marks the failings of someone or something.

I believe God was preparing, cleansing, and purifying His servant from any blemish, shame, or idolatry that he might have adopted while living in the land of Egypt. He was giving him a new life, a new beginning. Soon the Commander of the army of the Lord appeared to him, and Joshua fell to his knees and worshiped Him, asking, "What does my Lord say to His servant?" (verse 14). "Then the Commander of the army of the Lord said to him, 'Take your sandal off your foot, for the place where you stand is holy" (verse 15), and Joshua obeyed. Joshua was a warrior, an army general, so God, ever a relational God, came to him as the Commander of the Lord's army.

In the New Testament, the Lord God came to earth in such a way that He could relate to everyone. He took on flesh, coming to earth as one of us. Though He was fully human, He was also fully God. In the flesh, He conquered all sin by obeying and using God's Word. Empowered by the Holy Spirit, He became like one of us, teaching us the ways of God, showing us the character of God, and teaching us the way to live a life of dominion and power. By His coming to the earth, He was made lower than the angels, but He was more powerful because He was connected to God at all times. He used His empowerment to defeat in the flesh all obstacles, teaching us that if we submit ourselves to God our Father and obey Him in all things, we can do the same. In fact,

Jesus said that even greater things we would do than what He did (John 14:12). If you don't believe that, then maybe your faith is smaller than a mustard seed.

Jesus was so powerful because He was always connected to God the Father in every step He took and in every word He spoke. In everything He did, He acknowledged God and gave Him all praise, honor, and glory. He healed the sick, resurrected the dead, fed multitudes out of little, and rebuked demons, wind, and storms.

Jesus was so humble that He did not part the waters of the Sea of Galilee. He did something new, something simpler. He just walked on them, making full use of the power given to Him by God the Father.

Jesus has given us the same command as the one given to Moses and Joshua: we too must take the sandals off our feet. The wording is different, but the meaning is the same. He said, "If anyone desires to come after Me, let him deny himself, and take up his cross daily, and follow Me" (Luke 9:23). He has issued an open invitation to whoever wants to follow Him and be a part of Him.

Are you up to that challenge to walk daily in His presence?

Your Walk

Leading a men's group for many years has been a privilege for me. I love to see the transformation of lives that takes place. When a man's heart is transformed, everything in his life changes. He becomes a better dad, husband, friend, and leader.

One day as I was checking the fan page for my book *Reencounter with Jesus,* I noticed that it had over fifty thousand likes. To my surprise, I noted that 35 percent of the people engaged were between the ages of thirteen and seventeen, 58 percent were between the ages of eighteen and twenty-four, and only 7 percent were between the ages of thirty-five to sixty-five.

When I saw that, I thought to myself, *I have been investing my time with the wrong group!* I observed that teens and young adults are apparently hungrier for the Lord. They want to know about the true God. They are looking for answers, longing to belong and be a part of something. As leaders, we need to be available to lead and mentor them. These young people are the future leaders of this country, the future leaders of the world. They are the future doctors, engineers, athletes, songwriters, and moviemakers. We need to teach them about God and His commands so they can go into the marketplace, knowing and walking with the Lord. In that way, we can have a brighter tomorrow.

For the last two years, God has put in my path young people, like Tommy in this book, so that I might teach them the ways of the Lord. Previously, their only teachers have been the TV and the Internet. Disney has done a great deal of work to influence kids, so why not us? Disney understands that kids are gifted, and they condition them to do what they want them to do. In turn, many of them get lost in the pleasures of the world because they were never taught solid teaching about life and the giver of life.

There are also many gifted kids in church, but they are not being taught solid teaching. Instead, they are just being entertained. They are not given the opportunity to develop their gifts, talents, and abilities; as a result, they end up hiding their God-given talents.

There are many kids who are in the same situation as Tommy. They don't feel like going to church because of religion. They are hungry for the truth, but there is no one to lead them properly.

Moses was called to free God's people from oppression. Joshua freed the Israelites from bondage and disobedience. Jesus' disciples were called to free people from spiritual bondage. We are called to rescue our families, our marriages, our kids, our communities, our country, and even the world in order to turn them to the Lord.

We can jump, shout, dance, sing, preach, and fall out all night long, but until we are willing to take our sandals off and surrender completely to Him, we will not be able to execute His orders. When your heart is right, clean, and pure, you will not be satisfied to stand at a distance and just talk about the love, grace, and power of God. You will be compelled to live it. But for that to happen, you need to take your shoes off and walk on the holy ground He has laid before you. That holy ground was prepared by the blood of the Lamb, the Lord Jesus Christ.

It's time to surrender all and walk with God. Some of you have been waiting for a moment like this, waiting for a spark to fire you up to walk holy before God. Are you willing to take your sandals off your feet and draw closer to the burning presence of the glory of the Lord? Are you willing to stand in the brilliance of God's power and allow Him to guide and empower you to go wherever He commands? Are you ready for your new journey to walk daily in God's presence?

May the love of God the Father, the grace of the Lord Jesus Christ, and the communion of the Holy Spirit be with you.

We'd love to hear from you. Please share your walk with us at www.ReencouterWithJesus.com.

Acknowledgments

For many years, I sought to walk with God daily. When that day came, what a joy it was to wake up in the morning and know that the Lord was already there. Lord, what a joy it is to be able to talk to You, listen to You, and thank You for Your love and kindness. My heart fills with gladness when I experience Your presence and Your peace.

God, You are amazing! I thank You for entrusting me with this message and giving me the ability to put it into writing. I remember the first time You called me to write. I went forth without knowing what I was doing, but You took me by the hand and showed me all I needed to do. Thank You for guiding me and sending me as a minister of Your entrusting. To You, I give all honor, praise, and glory forever and ever.

To my gorgeous wife, Gloria, thank you for your support, your patience, and unconditional love.

To my little princess, Krystin, like always, you are my joy. I love you! God has so much prepared for you. Keep up the great work.

I want to thank my mom and dad for introducing me to the ways of the Lord when I was only seven years old. Since then, I have developed a passion to know God on a daily basis. Thank you for being obedient to His calling.

To author Justin Hart, thank you for your encouragement, coaching, and support. When I had no one to share my secret with, the first manuscript that God entrusted to me, you were there, sharing your wisdom with me, and you are still there for me.

To Nery Schelenker-Espinosza and her husband, Troy, thank you for your help and for having a pure heart in the work of the Lord and in service to others.

Special thanks to Pastor Derek Watson and his lovely wife, Maggie. When I first met you, you received me as if we had known each other forever. Thank you for your friendship and support. I pray every pastor and every leader in the world develops a heart as pure as yours.

A special thanks to all the staff at Westbow Press. Thank you for supporting this new message and for your professional, kind, and endless help.

To all of you who have been called to *take your sandals off,* may the Lord God continue to guide and empower you on your personal walk in His presence.